How to Start, Run and **Succeed** in your own Business

Derek Jones
Director, The Small Business Centre,
University of Aston

and

W. H. Perry
Senior Consultant, The Small Business Centre,
University of Aston

Wheatsheaf Books

Distributed by Harvester Press

First published in Great Britain in 1983 by
WHEATSHEAF BOOKS LTD
A MEMBER OF THE HARVESTER PRESS GROUP
Publisher: John Spiers
Director of Publications: Edward Elgar
16 Ship Street, Brighton, Sussex

Reprinted 1983, 1984, 1985

British Library Cataloguing in Publication Data

Jones, Derek
How to start, run and *Succeed* in your own business
1. Small business——Great Britain——Management
I. Title II. Perry, W. H.
658'.022'0941 HD69.S6

ISBN 0–7108–0159–9
ISBN 0–7108–0200–5 Pbk

Typeset in New Times Roman 10 pt on 12 pt by
South End Typographics, Pondicherry
and printed and bound in Great Britain by
Biddles Ltd, Guildford and King's Lynn

THE HARVESTER PRESS PUBLISHING GROUP
The Harvester Press Publishing Group comprises Harvester Press Limited (chiefly publishing literature, fiction, philosophy, psychology, science and trade books), Harvester Press Microform Publications Limited (publishing in microform unpublished archives, scarce printed sources, and indexes to these collections) and Wheatsheaf Books Limited (a wholly independent company chiefly publishing in economics, international politics, sociology and related social sciences), whose books are distributed by The Harvester Press Limited and its agencies throughout the world.

How to Start, Run and **Succeed** in your own Business

Contents

Preface

This book is written primarily to assist those people who are thinking of starting up a business, but it should prove equally useful to those who have already started their new venture and are now seeking further guidance. It applies equally to the businessman and businesswoman and their male and female employees. But to avoid endless repitition, the terms businessman and he are used. It deals in a simple practical way with the commercial, legal and control aspects of operating the small business. It does not purport to answer all the questions which the larger organisation may wish to pose. Neither does it attempt to replace the numerous specialist books dealing with such topics as marketing, book-keeping, accountancy, the law, and the management of people.

Time will, of course, bring about changes not only in the business opportunities available and the desire of people to take advantage of them, but also in many of the statutory requirements with which the businessman has to comply. These changes will inevitably lead in time to some of the statements made in various chapters of the book becoming out-of-date. For this reason it would be prudent for any owner or manager to consult the appropriate adviser whenever taking any major decisions concerning the future conduct of the business. This is especially true when embarking on any course of action when the owner or manager has any doubts about the legal implications of such actions.

1 Preliminary Steps

Running your own business can be not only a profitable but also a satisfying occupation. Many enterprising persons have launched out on their own and have built sound businesses which now provide them with a very good standard of living and pride of achievement. Unhappily many others who have set out with equally high ambitions have found that their business has not been the success they hoped for. It may even have ended in the liquidator's hands.

The reasons why some ventures succeed while others fail are many and varied. A few may owe their initial success to good luck – perhaps to having available goods or services for which an unexpectedly large demand suddenly arises. Some may have failed because of apparent ill-luck – the shopkeeper relying on a steady trade provided by the employees of a nearby large factory might be forced out of business by the unexpected closure of that factory. But these are the exceptions. The large majority of successes are the result of effective management, which means that the owner manages the business in such a way that customers' needs are met, while at the same time the available resources of money, materials, people and equipment are used profitably. This calls for careful forethought by an owner who sets realistic aims for the venture, makes plans to achieve them, and exercises firm control to make sure the business stays on course. Even the firm which gets off to a good start by having a lucky break in the early days must subsequently be properly managed if it is to succeed in the long term. On the other hand a very large number of firms fail because they have not been managed effectively. Instead of clear aims, the owner has over-optimistic or vague hopes, planning is replaced by short term and *ad hoc* decisions, and control is non-existent. Even the apparent bad luck of the shopkeeper, in our example, could well have been the result of a lack of forethought in relying so heavily on one source of trade.

Are You the Right Person?

Subsequent chapters of this book deal with the practical aspects of setting-up and managing the business in such a way that the chances of success are improved, and the risk of failure is reduced. Before looking at these aspects, however, it is well to look first at the type of person who appears most likely to make a success of setting up and operating a business in the long term. Our experience suggests that these are some of the features common to most successful owners:

Clear personal objectives
Dedication
Skills – practical and commercial
Willingness to learn
Ability to delegate
Judgement
Enthusiasm.

Clear personal objectives

Most successful business people started out with a very clear idea of what they wanted to achieve in life, and a very clear idea of how the business would help in achieving those aims. These may include, for example:

Independence,
Financial rewards higher than those obtainable from work as an employee,
Satisfying a creative urge,
Ensuring a secure future for the family,
Making fuller use of special skills.

An essential preliminary step for the potential businessman therefore is to clarify and define precisely these personal objectives; only then will it be possible to establish what it is that the business must achieve to realise these objectives. Needless to say, the identification of these personal objectives will not, of itself, ensure the success of the business. The ability to manage its affairs competently is equally crucial. However, without such clear definition, the business will lack positive direction and firm control. Those individuals who merely have a vague feeling that it would be a good idea to start up on their own, perhaps with the vision of an easy life ahead, would be well advised to abandon the idea and work for someone else.

Dedication

There are very few businesses which, in their early days, do not make great demands on the owner's time, family and social life, and nervous energy. It is not uncommon to find that people work perhaps twelve hours a day, six days a week until the future of the enterprise appears reasonably secure. Many owners have found that their business demands this degree of commitment for at least the first three to five years. But while remaining dedicated, the successful person must be able to meet these demands without becoming the victim of undue worry. Worry which leads to sleepless nights is bound to reduce the individual's effectiveness, and the habitual worrier is unlikely to become a successful businessman.

Skills

Frequently the founder of a firm has a special skill which is required in providing the goods or services being offered. This is especially true of the firm offering a personal service – hairdressing, electrical installation, or repairs to body-work of motor cars, where the founder has a high level of craft or professional ability. It is also true of most types of manufacture – reproduction furniture or plastic mouldings. However, in all types of business, there is need of more than practical or technical ability however valuable these may be. To be successful the owner must also exercise a range of skills which will ensure the commercial prosperity of the firm. For example, in the manufacturing business the owner must have or develop the skills of marketing, controlling the finances of the firm, planning and controlling production, and managing people. Almost certainly this means that most people starting a business for the first time will have new skills to learn.

Willingness to learn

It is characteristic of most people who have made a success of their business that they have had the foresight to identify which skills or knowledge they lacked, and have taken steps to remedy these deficiencies. In this process they may have taken the opportunity to learn from professional advisers, attended schools or colleges, or even taken temporary employment where the necessary skill could be developed to the appropriate level. They have been ready to learn from their business associates and, as the business has grown, from their own employees.

Ability to delegate

In the early days the entrepreneur may run the enterprise single-handed, or with a few assistants. However, if the business is to grow, the owner must be able to delegate some responsibilities to well-chosen employees. The business where the boss does not delegate cannot grow beyond the size where everything can be controlled in detail by one person.

Judgement

The head of a small firm is continually taking decisions which affect the business in both the short and long term. These usually have to be taken with little or no assistance from colleagues or outside advisers and judgement is called for in distinguishing between major and minor decisions. It is important to recognise those decisions which can affect the survival or growth of the firm, and to devote to them the time and thought necessary to ensure a proper balance between short-term benefits and long-term prospects. The minor decisions call for judgement in deciding how much time it is worth spending on collecting and analysing information before taking the decision. The person who takes snap decisions on all matters runs the risk of making major mistakes which can ruin the business. On the other hand, the person who spends too long on minor decisions may miss opportunities which would be beneficial to the business.

Enthusiasm

This is the positive quality which helps to keep the individual dedicated to the task, even in times of difficulty. It may arise from a firm belief in the quality of the product or service, from keenness to exercise a special skill, or even a strong desire for personal gain. Whatever the source, enthusiasm is a stimulant to the owner, and will probably be communicated to other people whom he meets in the normal course of business.

Business Objectives

It is important that the future businessman establishes clear objectives for the business which will enable him to realise personal aims. For example, the person developing a new product will probably have a definite target date for marketing the product, and a target for level of sales within a defined period. The size of the annual profit may be of secondary importance as long as the job provides the satisfaction of achievement. On the other hand, if the personal objective is large financial gain, the entrepreneur will set financial objectives which include large profits, possibly at the expense of the personal satisfaction which would accrue from exercising practical or technical skills in less profitable ventures.

What is certain is that whatever the personal objectives are, the business must have two clear financial objectives. First, there must be profits at a level which will enable the business to survive in the long run, and to meet the owner's personal objectives. Secondly, there must always be enough cash available to enable the business to survive in the short term. Then, having set these objectives, plans must be made to achieve them, and procedures devised to monitor the firm's progress towards them.

Later we shall describe in detail practical steps to meet these requirements. At this stage it is enough to emphasise the importance of establishing objectives, plans and procedures from the very start. An interesting example of the value of this approach is provided by a company known to the authors, which was set up by three people who had identified a market for a particular textile product. Before selling, making any of the product, or even finding premises, they carried out a thorough research of the market, prepared a detailed budget for sales, expenditure and profit for the first year, and made outline plans for the two following years. At this stage they felt confident about going ahead. This they did to such effect that not only was the first year's objective achieved, but they were also able to keep to the plans for the following years with only minor modifications. These people knew what they wanted to achieve, verified that their aims were realistic, and exercised the skills of management in achieving their success.

Service, Retail, Wholesale or Manufacture

Some people who are attracted to the idea of self-employment in itself, may not yet have decided on the type of business they would like to go into. Broadly speaking the choice is between four major categories:

Service,
Retail,
Wholesale and
Manufacture.

Some businesses do not fit neatly into any one of these divisions – for example, the bakery which supplies outside customers as well as having its own front shop is in retail and manufacturing. Nevertheless, if we deal with these four categories separately it should help the potential owner to assess the advantages and drawbacks of the possible businesses he has in mind.

Service

This covers a wide range of activities. In addition to professional people (not discussed here as we may assume they have already decided their future sphere of action), we find such services as: electricians, motor-car repairers, hirers of vehicles or equipment, maintenance and cleaning services, catering, secretarial services, and many others.

While some service businesses call for considerable capital, in addition to special skills – the hire of equipment for example – the majority demand some special skill but relatively little capital. Quite often the person's skill and a few tools and pieces of equipment are all that are required to make a start, and this may be the right way for people with skills to start, especially if those skills are in short supply. It is usually less advisable for people without special skills – if they can do the job then many others can also do it, and competition might be quite fierce.

Retail

The would-be shopkeeper needs capital for stock, premises and fittings, so retailing may not be a possible choice for those without access to capital. In addition, the successful retail operation calls for several skills – marketing, stock control, and financial control, as well as a sound knowledge of the goods to be sold. Most small shopkeepers must also be able to offer something the big competitors cannot match. This may be service – perhaps keeping the shop open after normal closing hours – or it may be specialist advice not available at the supermarket or chain-store. No person intending to open a small shop should necessarily expect to compete on price with the bigger outlets.

A word of warning is necessary to anyone who intends specialising in a product with seasonal demand, such as children's toys. The departmental or chain-stores will often make a practice of stocking these items only during the busy season, and then offer them at prices below those which the specialist has to charge. They can do this because the resources and space allocated to these goods during the season can be re-allocated to other goods at other times. The specialist, on the other hand, might have to rely on sales during the busy season to cover most of the annual cost.

The shopkeeper who intends to do more than just make a living will find that his business demands a great deal of time. Apart from being on duty during opening hours, there will be the daily checking and banking of cash, frequent checks of stock, placing orders to replenish the store room and shelves, keeping up-to-date the books of account, and keeping any records which may be demanded by national or local government. It can add up to a very full day, and no one who is not prepared to devote this amount of time to the business should consider being a shopkeeper.

Wholesaling

This term may be used to describe a wide range of activities all of which have one feature in common – they are solely concerned with buying a product from a supplier and supplying it to a commercial user or trader. Obviously the small business will not try to compete with large wholesalers offering a wide range of goods, but many people have built up successful businesses by specialising in one product or a small range of products – for example, photographic equipment. They have developed a special relationship with a few suppliers, and established a reputation with a number of regular customers. Often the business depends on being the sole importer (or one of very few) of a product for which there is a steady but not large demand. The successful people in this kind of activity usually have a good knowledge of the product, or of opportunities in the market.

Unless the operation is purely factoring, – buying and selling without actually handling the goods – a fairly large amount of capital will be required to buy and hold stocks, and to provide premises for storage. The skills called for are similar to those of the retailer.

Manufacturing

The potential manufacturer needs capital and business skills, and must either have technical and practical skills, or be able to recruit someone with these skills. Business skills are needed because the manufacturer has to plan and control a wide variety of activities – sales, production, distribution and buying – at the same time keeping firm financial control and motivating people. The business might be set up either to make its own products (in which case skills of design may also be needed), or to offer a sub-contracting service, that is, making components for a larger manufacturer. An own-product offers the advantage that production may be planned for smooth, steady operation with goods being made for stock during periods when sales are slack.

There might also be more latitude in price-fixing. The own-product firm could well be offering a benefit to customers not matched by competitors – better quality goods, a new product, or superior technical advice. The sub-contracting firm, on the other hand, perhaps supplying products to a set design and specification, will probably meet fierce price competition. It might find that profits are hard to come by unless it can offer a better service – prompt delivery, readiness to meet customers' (often unreasonable) demands, and so on – than that provided by competitors.

The sub-contracting business has the advantage that there should be relatively little capital tied up in finished goods: as soon as the goods have been made they can be despatched and invoices rendered. The own-product business has to tie up funds in maintaining an adequate stock of finished goods to anticipate the probable demands of customers.

In either type of business, the person with a good experience of manufacturing industry will have a good start over rivals without this experience.

Getting Started

Before proceeding with the venture the potential owner must, by detailed and comprehensive investigation, be satisfied that there is a market for the product, and that the business has a real chance of gaining an adequate share of the market. (Chapter 2 deals with the whole subject of marketing in some detail.) At this stage we shall confine our attention to the questions which must be answered before the venture can get under way:

Is there a market for the goods or services?
Who are the customers in this market?
How many of these customers should I expect to attract?
What competition already exists?
What price can realistically be charged?

Is there a market?

There can be little doubt that a market exists for the services of the painter-decorator, or the goods offered by the retailer of baby clothes, or pottery products for example. It may not be so obvious that a market exists for a new do-it-yourself gadget, a specialist magazine, or a high-class lunch-box service. If there is any doubt, it is necessary to find out if a market already exists or, failing that, if one could be created. The work involved could be quite time-consuming, but is essential before going any further with the project.

Who are the customers?

The next step is to identify the different types of customer in the market. For example, the plumber has the choice of industrial companies or private householders, or perhaps house-builders if his skills include advising on and installing heating- and ventilating-systems. The ornamental iron-worker may supply direct to the householder or sell to retailing outlets. On the other hand, the appeal of a lunch-box service might be limited to the employees of commercial and industrial premises.

How many customers?

If the market exists and its customers have been identified, the next question is whether there are enough potential customers to meet the firm's sales objectives, and if so, whether a sufficient number can be persuaded to buy the service or goods on offer at a price which yields adequate profit.

What competition exists?

This question follows on from the previous one, as the presence of competitors must influence the number of customers who can be attracted. There is another consideration, too – the possible existence of competing products. For example, the inventor of the new do-it-yourself gadget might find that the potential users' needs are already being met by a cheaper product performing the same function. Thus no matter how brilliant the idea, the product is unlikely to attract many buyers.

What selling price?

For a business to survive and prosper, the goods or services offered must be able to command a price which will yield a profit from the volume of sales achieved. This might seem so obvious as not to need saying. However, many businesses have failed by not observing this simple rule; they have aimed at volume of sales rather than at profit. The question of price therefore resolves itself into three further questions:

What is the customer prepared to pay?
What revenue will that price yield at the volume of planned sales?
What costs will be involved in providing that volume of sales?

These questions are dealt with in detail in chapters 2 and 9. Meanwhile it is important for the prospective entrepreneur to remember that the final arbiter on price is the customer, unless the product or service offered has a monopoly of the market. The new small business is unlikely to find itself in this happy position.

Although the five original questions posed have been dealt with separately, they are of course related. There might be a market for the goods or services, but the price which the owner must charge might not attract enough customers to make the business profitable. There may already be competitors offering a high quality service and good value, making it difficult for the new firm to get established. Or there might be an existing competitive product which virtually puts the market out of reach because it offers more value at the same price, or equal value at a lower price. Nevertheless, enough customers may be attracted if a better product or service can be offered, albeit at a higher price. If after having answered all the questions it is clear that the product or service is unlikely to attract enough custom at the right price it would be unwise to proceed with the venture.

Premises

Having identified a potential market for the service or product the entrepreneur will need premises from which to operate. The two questions to answer are:

What kind of premises?
Where should they be located?

Type of premises

The type of premises naturally depends on the nature of the work.

The person offering a service which is always carried out on customers' premises – the painter and decorator – might be able to manage quite well working from home. Before setting up in this way, it is essential to check that there are no restrictive clauses in any tenancy or ownership agreements which would prevent this. In addition, local authority regulations may impose constraints on the type of activity which may be carried out, or materials which may be stored on the premises. There may also be other restrictions (and this applies to all types of premises) limiting permissible noise levels, the emission of fumes, smoke and waste gases or the discharge of undesirable chemicals or other waste matter into rivers or public sewers.

If the option of working from home is chosen it is advisable to set aside one room, provided with a telephone, to be used solely for business and not for domestic purposes. This ensures that all books of account, business correspondence, diaries or engagement books, drawings, plans, catalogues, etc. are kept apart from personal possessions. It also ensures that any business associates can be received in surroundings which convey an impression that they are dealing with a businesslike firm.

The retailer will be looking for shop premises suitable not only for displaying the merchandise but also for storing adequate stock in appropriate conditions. An office will be essential for keeping records and other papers associated with the business.

The manufacturer will require premises providing a workroom, storage and office space. If the work calls for the use of heavy machinery, equipment, materials or components it will be essential to check that the structure and floor are strong enough to cope with the load to be placed on it. Expert advice will probably be necessary.

Whatever the type of business a choice has to be made between renting, leasing or buying. The obvious advantage of renting or leasing is that less capital will be required initially. It has the drawback that tenure will probably be for a limited period at the end of which rents might be increased, or the tenancy terminated so that the firm has to move. Buying premises freehold or with a long lease will provide security of tenure, but will involve extra capital at the outset. A short lease will probably be cheaper, but carries the possibility of an enforced move when the lease expires.

Location

The potential owner might, for personal reasons, wish to site the business in a particular area, but it would be a coincidence if this also happened to be the best location for the business. Local regulations may limit the type of business which can be established in certain streets, or the use to which certain premises may be put, so a choice has to be made, or a balance struck, between personal preferences and the needs of the business. Among the questions to ask, with the interests of the business in view, are:

Where are the potential customers?
Where are the potential competitors?
What is the main source of materials?
What skilled employees are needed?
Are adequate transport services available for goods and people?
Does the business need special electricity, gas or water supplies?

The retailer's main concern is with his customers. If the chosen activity relies on passing trade – the newsagent and tobacconist, for example – then obviously the shop should be in a busy shopping area where there are a large number of potential customers. If the business is aiming at a specialist market, for example, supplying sheet music and musical instruments, it could probably operate at a lower cost in a quieter area. This type of firm will attract its customers by suitable publicity and subsequent good service, thus building up a regular clientele to whom the location is of minor importance.

The retailer must also be concerned with the location of his competitors. Many types of business are better sited at a distance from others of the same type. The small ironmonger's shop comes into this category. On the other hand, some shops may attract more custom if sited near other shops associated with their type of product or service. This applies to greengroceries, bakeries and butchers.

The person offering a service involving visits to customers will wish to be as near to potential customers as possible, to limit travelling time to the job.

The firm offering a service to be carried out on its own premises – motor-car servicing for example – should be located where customers find it easy to call in – either near their homes or their place of work.

Many manufacturers may be less concerned with proximity to customers than with other factors, including access to good road and rail services and the location of suppliers of bulky materials. If it is proposed to engage employees, the supply of people with suitable skills will also be important. And in rural areas, it may be essential to locate the workshop on a site which already has adequate electricity and gas services, otherwise the expense of installing these facilities might be prohibitive.

At this point a word of warning is appropriate to those who are considering setting up in a rural area simply because it is a pleasant place to live in. Many firms which have set up in such areas have found that capital costs, including provision of power and other services, have been high and that the distance of the firm from major customers has hampered their selling activities. They have also found that some of their operating costs – especially transport and telephones – have been high, and in consequence they have had to be satisfied with lower profits than similar firms in industrial areas. (These comments do not, of course, apply to such activities as supply and repair of agricultural machinery which must, by the location of their customers, be situated in rural areas.)

In these few paragraphs we have not attempted to produce a comprehensive guide. However enough has probably been said to indicate that the location of premises merits as much careful study as the other considerations dealt with.

How Much Capital?

Whatever type of business is envisaged, the potential owner will need cash to get the venture under way. Chapter 3 deals with this question in some detail. In this general survey of essential preliminary steps it is enough to make two points. First, any forecasts must tend towards the pessimistic side rather than the optimistic. In other words, in addition to the total which has been arrived at by careful research and analysis to cover all foreseeable needs, an allowance – perhaps 10 per cent or more – should be added to allow for those events, unforeseen but inevitable, which will make demands upon the funds. Secondly, there will probably be a period (perhaps several months) during which the business will have little or no income. During this time the proprietor and his family must live, so an adequate allowance must be made for living and personal expenses.

These calculations might show that funds available from personal sources will fail to meet the needs of the business. Thought must then be given to external sources – partners, bank loans, state or local grants, etc. The source of funds can have an important bearing on who eventually controls the business, so this aspect must be very carefully investigated.

The Form of the Business

Before starting to trade, the owner must decide whether he will operate as a sole trader, or in partnership with another person or persons, or be incorporated with limited liability. The essential difference between these forms lies in the degree of liability undertaken by the owner(s). The person of the sole trader cannot be separated from the business, they are one and the same, and all liabilities of the business are treated as liabilities of the person. Thus failure of the business could result in loss of all personal property and fortune.

Similarly, the partners in a partnership are individually and collectively liable for all the debts of the partnership. The company which has been incorporated with limited liability, however, is a separate entity from the owners. For this reason the liability of the owners is limited to the nominal value of the shares which they have taken in the company. Their personal fortune is thus not directly at risk. It should be borne in mind, however, that this apparent advantage is sometimes illusory. During the early months of the life of the company it might be necessary to arrange credit with suppliers for goods or materials, or to arrange an overdraft or loan with a bank, or to raise a loan from other sources. If this is the case the creditor, bank or lender may ask for security in the form of a personal guarantee. This effectively removes the limitation from liability and the owner is in the same position as the sole trader or partners. This is dealt with in more detail in later chapters.

Advisers

However competent they may be, very few people starting out on their own will be able to get their business under way without help from three specialists: the bank manager, the accountant, the solicitor.

The bank manager

A good bank manager can advise on many commercial and business matters not necessarily those limited to finance. He should have a good knowledge of local affairs and business establishments. He will probably have the backing of a central information and advice service. The intelligent owner will keep the bank manager fully informed of his plans for the business and of its progress. In return the bank manager should be able and willing to offer sound advice as well as financial help.

The accountant

The form in which a business is set up will determine whether or not it is required by law to prepare and submit annual accounts and a balance sheet to the appropriate authority. If it is required to do so, the accounts must be audited by a qualified member of an accounting body authorised by legislation to undertake this duty.

Many business, however, are initially set up in a form which does not involve statutory submission of such accounts. The owner may therefore consider that the services of an accountant can be dispensed with. It should be borne in mind, however, that properly prepared accounts may be valuable for other purposes – they provide reliable evidence of the results of trading for tax or other officials; accounts drawn up professionally by a qualified, independent accountant are likely to carry more weight than accounts drawn up by the owner. Further, the accountant should be able to advise the owner on how to arrange the firm's financial affairs so that liability for tax is legally kept to a minimum. For these reasons alone the fees paid for this service will be justified by the saving of the owner's time in negotiating with officialdom, and the direct cash saving in taxes.

There is an even more important reason. An accountant with wide experience in industry or commerce will be able to prepare accounts in such a manner that they regularly provide valuable, up-to-date information concerning the activities and results of the business. This means that the owner can take important decisions based on knowledge rather than guesswork. Accounts prepared in this way are termed *management accounts*.

Some accountants specialise in auditing and preparing accounts for statutory purposes. Others specialise in providing information to facilitate the proper management of the business. Many cover both fields, and these provide best value to the small firm. The owner might be fortunate enough to find an independent accountant of this type, or it might be necessary to use the service of a practice whose members cover the whole field.

Later chapters in this book deal with the subject of management accounts. After reading these sections the owner will have a clearer idea of the kind of information the firm needs and how often it is needed. Armed with this knowledge it will be easier to approach both individual accountants and practices to assess whether or not they can meet the owner's needs. Most competent professionals are happy to co-operate by answering any questions concerning their services, and are likely to appreciate the opportunity of working for a firm which knows what it wants. Business acquaintances may also be able to offer useful advice on the services they receive from their own accountants. These services will cost more than simple auditing. But the extra cost should be recovered many times over by the improved profitability of the business. In the authors' experience, proper advice on these lines has led to the development of many successful businesses; and lack of advice or poor advice has frequently led to failure.

A word of caution may be appropriate here to the owner who has decided to use the services of an accountant. Remember it is your business; you must decide how it is to be run and what information you need. Take advice from your accountant, but make sure you thoroughly understand all the implications of his advice and the meaning of the accounting jargon. Then take the decision yourself.

The solicitor

The prudent owner will make sure he has a competent solicitor to advise him. The vast volume of legislation concerning industry and commerce is too wide in scope and too complex in detail for the busy owner to have time to understand it all. This complexity leads most lawyers to specialise in one of the many branches of the law: the small firm will probably require the service of a solicitor knowledgeable in commercial and employment law. Most family solicitors are not normally involved in these aspects, and the knowledge and experience required is more likely to be found in a firm of commercial solicitors, with partners who are specialists in different branches of the law. As with accountants, the services of the best adviser can be expensive, but the lack of specialist advice in the commercial or employment field could lead to very heavy losses. The right solicitor or firm is usually found by consulting business friends or advisers because their work most often comes to them by recommendation.

The Next Steps

The prospective entrepreneur is now ready to make plans for setting up and running the business. The following chapters deal with these in some detail, but it may be useful at this stage to list the steps which have to be taken:

(1) Establish how much cash is required to set up the business and meet running costs until money starts to flow in.
(2) Decide on the sources of this initial capital – personal funds, friends or relatives, partners, banks, national or local government grants, etc.
(3) Decide whether the firm is to be set up as a sole trader or partnership, or if it is to be a company with limited liability.
(4) Take any steps necessary to register with the appropriate authorities.
(5) Study local and national legislation relevant to the activities of the firm.
(6) Find suitable premises.
(7) Notify appropriate authorities and the Inland Revenue that the firm is about to start trading.

It is in taking these steps that the value of the bank mananger, accountant and solicitor will become apparent.

Two True Stories

The history of two firms, well known to the authors, illustrate many of the main points raised in this and subsequent chapters. One story is of success, the other of failure.

Mr and Mrs A. some twenty years ago, and with a capital of a few hundred pounds, set up a company to make metal components for the building and electrical industries. Their technical knowledge of the trade was limited, but they had some experience of the market. They started with a few simple, second-hand machines in a rented shed, and found a number of customers who gave them orders for sub-contract work. As a team of two they quoted for contracts, bought materials, produced the components, invoiced the customers, and chased for payment. As business increased they were able to employ people to work the machines, and take some of the load of actually producing the components off their hands.

Then they moved into larger premises and engaged a qualified engineer to take responsibility for technical matters and supervise production. The business continued to grow, and today they are operating in a modern factory, with the most up-to-date machinery and office equipment available. They still employ fewer than fifty employees, but sales turnover is equal to that of similar companies two or three times their size. Profitability measured by the conventional measures of return on capital, and return on sales or profit per employee is well above the average for the industry. Competent managers now attend to day-to-day activities so that the owners are able, while keeping overall control, to plan the future development of the business.

How have they achieved this success? Right from the start they had clear financial aims and plans. They dedicated all their working hours for some years to the needs of the business – sixty- or seventy-hour weeks were not uncommon. Equally important, they kept a tight control of all activities. Customers, while being treated courteously, were not allowed to take extended credit; the quality of service offered enabled the company to be very firm in demanding payment. A very close watch was kept on costs, and even in the very early days they set up a procedure for recording costs for comparison with estimates. With the help of advisers they set up a system for control of production. They set up financial reporting procedures which helped them keep a close watch on profit. They kept their mix of customers under review to avoid over-reliance on any one customer or industry. While doing all this they gave much thought to the recruitment of suitable employees and the establishment of good conditions of work, so that grievances have been few, and the staff is well-motivated. In particular, supervisors and managers have been most carefully selected both for their competence and ability to fit into the team.

Needless to say it has not all been plain sailing. Mistakes have been made, some customers have complained, some costs have been excessive, some managers have failed and left, and there have been minor grievances among the employees. But the owners have always been ready to learn from experience and to take advice, either from their own staff or external advisers.

Perhaps the best testimony to the success of such methods is provided by the fact that during two serious depressions the company has survived in good shape, and has prospered while other firms in the same industry have been forced to close.

The other story is of a man with practical experience of manufacturing who saw an opening in serving the leisure industry. His contact with a caravan manufacturer led to his taking an order to provide certain fitments, for which purpose he set up a small workshop and employed three or four people. Cash came from his own resources to fund the original purchase of material and pay his employees.

First deliveries were made and payment was received one month later, accompanied by an order for an increased quantity of fitments. More material was bought and production stepped up. The business continued to operate for some months, with deliveries being made and substantial orders received. Then, quite unexpectedly, the customer failed to pay at the usual time and requested a temporary hold-up in deliveries as sales were falling off. When a request for payment was made the reply was that the customer had no cash and was unlikely to be able to pay for several months. The entrepreneur approached his bank manager with a request for an overdraft or loan but this was refused, and the promising young company had to close.

Why did it fail? First, the owner had not taken a long-term view and had no clear objectives. He seized the opportunity for short-term profitability without careful assessment of the market and had no plans for the longer-term. Next, he allowed his company to be tied to one customer. This is a weakness in any business. Even more important, he committed the business sin of over-trading – he took on more work than he could finance. He failed to plan and control his cash flows. If he had instituted a reporting procedure from the outset he would probably have declined the increased orders. He failed to seek the advice of his accountant and bank manager who could have guided him in these aspects. In sum, he failed to control the business and paid the penalty.

2 Marketing

We are now ready to look in more detail at some of the topics raised in chapter 1. The first subject to consider is the customer, without whom we have no business. Before we can launch our venture we must satisfy ourself that we can attract enough customers prepared to spend enough money on our goods or service to enable us to make the profit needed to meet our objectives. Then we have to decide how to reach these customers and sell enough goods or service at the right price. Finally, when the business is under way, we have to decide what steps to take to maintain or expand the volume of sales. These matters are the subject of this chapter and can be summed up in one word – *marketing*.

Finding the Customers

First of all we must ask ourselves if there are any customers at all for the product or service. For most types of business this question may be unnecessary, because there is already an obvious demand – the newsagent, electrician, or the supplier of components to the car manufacturer, for example. However, one occasionally meets the enthusiast with an idea who has sunk a lot of capital into a venture before checking that the product or service meets any real need however brilliant the idea may appear to be. These are the people who should really be asking this question, and doing a great deal of work to find the answer before going further.

How do they find out whether the idea is a commercial proposition? The detailed answer depends on the type of product or service. But in general terms they must establish who *might* be interested, make a list of possible customers, and then go and ask them. If the product is for industrial use many of the potential customers will be listed in directories such as *Kompass* (available in most public reference libraries) which provide names and addresses of firms, with information about their activities. Selected firms can then be approached to find out if they might be interested. This also applies to anyone offering a new service to industry. He has to list possible customers and find out if they have a use for the service. (If the service is intended for domestic customers the simplest and best approach may be to visit householders and ask if they are interested.) This research involves a lot of work, but it is vital to the success of the venture.

Who are the Customers?

The research so far will have established that there are customers for the goods or service. But this is not enough. First, have all the categories of possible customers been identified? Discussions with business acquaintances or friends might indicate customers not previously considered. (In this context, it maybe useful to join the local trade associations, Chamber of Commerce, etc.) Secondly, within the range of possible customers, which specific categories should the business be aiming at? Often the nature of the product or service points to the type of customer who needs it. For example, if the firm intends to import and sell a component for central heating systems there are at least four possible categories of customer plumbers, contractors, builders and do-it-yourself enthusiasts. The final choice will probably be made after further research has indicated which category appears to be most likely to help achieve the profit objective.

Alternatively, it may happen that the selected category of customer will help to decide the type of product or service to be offered. For example, the retailer of clothing has a wide range of customers to choose from – elderly or young, male or female, upper-class or middle-class, and a whole host of others. If the firm decides to aim at the young, well-off person, the clothes offered will probably have to be striking and colourful, and in line with current fashions.

The skilled person offering a service – the electrician or plumber, for example – has several categories to choose from. These might include maintenance work for industrial or commercial premises, repairs for householders, new work for the same customers, or installation work for builders. The carpenter/joiner who has decided to set up a manufacturing business may aim at one or more of several types of customer. Again the range is wide – supplying items for contract furnishers, making cabinets for television manufacturers, making special products for sale to department stores, and many others.

Whatever the business the same criterion must be used in making the choice. Which category of customer is most likely to provide the profit which ensures that the firm meets its objective?

What is the Demand?

Now that the potential customers have been defined, the next step is to find out whether the firm can sell enough to them to meet the profit target. This will depend on two factors:

(1) The size of the total market – that is, the amount of money being spent by all the customers (or likely to be spent by them) on the type of goods or service offered.
(2) The share of the market which the firm can expect to gain.

To establish the size of the market, two further questions have to be asked: How many potential customers are there? What quantities of the product are they likely to buy?

There is no one way which can guarantee a reliable, accurate answer, but some properly thought-out research will provide a better indication than unsupported hunches. The type of questions which a retailer (or person offering a service to private customers) should ask could be along these lines:

(1) In the possible trading areas, how many of the following are there? –
  Houses – upper-, middle-, lower-class
  Hotels – 1, 2, 3, 4, 5 star
  Offices – large, medium, small
  Shops – supermarkets, chain-stores, independents (large, medium, small)
  Factories – large, medium, small
(2) In each of these categories:
  How many people are there?
  How many have to shop outside the area in order to satisfy their needs?
  How many choose to shop outside the area and are able to travel to do so?
  What is the age range?
  What is the spending power?
  Is demand likely to be seasonal? If so, what percentage of the annual demand is seasonal? When and how long are the seasons?

As well as looking at the existing pattern, possible future developments of the area also need to be studied – proposed factories, housing estates, shops, offices, etc. On the other hand, a manufacturer intending to supply components to the motor-car trade may ask:

How many cars are produced each year in the United Kingdom?
How many replacements may be required for cars 3, 4, 5 years old, or more?
How many garages are there in the different regions of the country?
How many do-it-yourself shops are there?
Is there an overseas replacement market? If so, how large?

Deciding on the right questions needs a lot of thought, but finding the answers calls for a great deal of hard work. There are fortunately many sources of information available.

First there is the reference section of the public library. The person who can describe fairly precisely what information is required will usually find that the librarians can be of very great help. They are professionals in the art of locating sources of information and will often go to a great deal of trouble to provide the answers. The service is usually free. In some towns and cities a similar service is available at the local university or polytechnic.

A good starting point is to look for government publications and statistics; a very wide range exists. For example, if the firm is considering the supply of materials or a service to the building trade there are government publications called *Building, Construction and Property*. These publications give details of new housing programmes in the current period, whilst other related publications might include forecasts for future periods. Other examples of government publications are:

A regular statistical review of social trends.
Business monitors which provide information for more than 300 categories of industry, including for each industry:
- Total turnover
- Average costs
- Trends and seasonal patterns
- Analysis by the various sections of the industry.

Other sources of information are:

Trade associations for specific industries.
Commercial directories. A typical example is *Kompass*, which

gives detailed information of suppliers and their products and trade associations.

British Telecom. Yellow Pages and Green Pages.

Specialist directories (such as the *Retail Directory*) for particular industries.

Cuttings services (available in some reference libraries).

Reports of market research carried out by commercial research houses (sometimes available in reference libraries).

When all available information has been collected from these sources there will almost certainly be gaps which can only be filled by contact with potential customers. The usual practice is to select a representative sample from the appropriate directory and then ask for information in one of three ways: Postal questionnaires, telephone, or personal visit.

If the postal questionnaire method is used, experience shows that only about 5 per cent of people contacted will reply, so to get a reasonable sample it would be necessary to write to 1000 or more recipients. To increase the chances of a reply the questionnaire should be brief – one page only – easy to complete, and a reply paid envelope should be enclosed.

The telephone method calls for much tact, because a casual call may not be welcomed by the busy recipient. It is also costly and time-consuming. However, it is likely that about 50 per cent of the calls will produce a reasonable response so that a 100 or so calls might be adequate. The advantages of the method are that more searching questions can be put, and the status of the respondent can be established.

The best approach is probably by personal visit, preceded by a telephone call to make an appointment. A person who has agreed to the interview will be much more likley to provide reliable information, and the questioner will be able to probe more deeply into matters of interest. Even so, caution is called for when evaluating the replies. Some interviewees may give an over-optimistic impression of sales potential, because they have not thoroughly assessed their needs and do not wish to discourage the interviewer—and in any event they are not committed to buy the product or service subsequently.

When the size of the market has been assessed, the share which the firm can expect to gain is more difficult to determine. While some idea may have been gained during the research, it is probably better to approach the problem from another angle and ask: What share must my firm gain if the profit objective is to be reached? If the answer indicates that only a small share is needed, then the firm might have a good chance of getting it. If a very large share is required, it might be better to think again – of a different product or service, or of a different section of the market.

What Competition is There?

Information about competitors may be found in many of the sources used when finding potential customers – especially the relevant trade press, the Yellow Pages and the directories. In addition, the retailer will find that one of the best ways of getting information will be to walk around the chosen area and look, taking note of the shops in the same line of business, assessing their individual strengths and weaknesses, and observing which appear to be most popular. A person providing a service to local industry may get a good idea of strength of competition by approaching users of the service and finding out how satisfied they are. The manufacturer will probably make use of published information supplemented by discussions with members of any associations or similar bodies to which he has access.

Another useful source of information lies in the publicity material issued by competitors – leaflets, brochures, catalogues, etc. – which indicate the nature and specification of competing products or activities.

A new business attempting to enter an established market should expect some reaction from existing suppliers. The degree of reaction will depend largely on how important the particular market is to them. Where it contributes only a small percentage to total profits the competitor might not think it worth while taking strong defensive action. On the other hand, where it contributes a very high percentage, and this might well be so for a retailer or provider of a service in a small town, the reaction could take the form of extra publicity, price cutting and special promotions.

In general, it will often pay to analyse the degree to which present suppliers meet the needs of the customer. If it can be found that some needs are not being adequately satisfied at the moment – this may be a subjective judgement or based on real evidence – then a new business can place itself in a strong position by catering to those particular needs.

What is the Right Price?

There is one final question to ask in assessing whether or not the venture looks likely to succeed – this is, what price should be charged? The decision rests on two factors. The first is the price the customer is prepared to pay, and the second is the cost of providing the goods or service. During the survey of the market carried out earlier, the price which it will bear will probably have become clearer. Later, in chapter 9, the subject of costs is examined in relation to the minimum price which must be charged to achieve the planned profit. In the rather rare event that there is little or no competition (because of some scarce skill or new invention) there will be no established price level, and this is where judgement is called for. It might appear that the product would command a price yielding very much more than the target profit. But as this could attract competitors it might be more prudent to set the price at a level which would not invite competition, but would still yield a more than adequate profit.

Provided the answers to all the questions have been favourable, this ends the first task of the marketing exercise. (If the answers have not been favourable it will be necessary to try again, perhaps by looking at a different category of customer, or even a different product or service.)

Now the task begins of persuading the customers to buy. To do this one must first of all get the message to them that the product or service is on the market, and that it offers special benefits.

Persuading the Customer to Buy

Constructing the message

At this point it is helpful for the potential seller to try to put himself in the position of the potential buyer and ask: 'Why should I buy it?' The answer will provide a useful starting point from which to decide what the customer should be told. Some of the features which may provide the reason for the customer deciding on this product in preference to that of our competitors are:

Performance	Convenience
Economy	Prompt service or delivery
Price	Terms and conditions
Quality	Appearance

Safety or security	Status
Reliability	Pride of ownership
Guarantee	Potential for re-sale.

They will not all apply at the same time to any one individual product, but it should be possible, using the results of the previous research into customer attitudes and preferences, to select two or three which constitute the strongest, perhaps unique, selling points.

Now, using these points, it is a relatively straightforward task to develop the marketing message which will be used in the medium of publicity – advertisement, leaflets, etc. – which we choose. The message will summarise concisely but adequately the special benefits which the customer will enjoy from the goods or service. It will therefore be short and to the point, and written in the language the customer will understand (this might mean using non-technical language). This initial message will include only the key features of what benefits are offered, leaving embellishments and details to a later stage when customers have shown enough interest to make enquiries or start negotiations.

Getting the message to the customers

Means must now be found of getting this short, relevant, persuasive message to the customer. Several channels are open, and the choices available which are pertinent to the needs of the new venture include:

Leaflets
Advertising in newspapers, journals, etc.
Mail shots
Brochures and catalogues
Exhibitions
Local radio
Editorial features in newspapers, radio or television
Personal contacts.

The best medium to choose will depend on many factors – the kind of product or service offered, the type of customers and their location, and the type of message. Consider a firm set up by a highly skilled motor mechanic and panel beater whose special selling points are high quality work and collection of motor-cars from customers' homes. For this firm a simple leaflet, run-off on a copying machine and delivered through the letter boxes in a nearby residential district, might have a greater effect than a professionally

– produced brochure or an advertisement in the local press. On the other hand, the inventor of a product using advanced technology might decide that the best ways of reaching the limited range of possible customers include professionally-produced brochures, the trade press and exhibitions.

Leaflets The single-sheet leaflet offers a very effective means by which the retailer or provider of a new service may announce the opening of the business to people in the locality. The leaflets may be distributed by the proprietor of the business, by assistants specially recruited for the task, or by local newsagents. This process should be repeated regularly to keep the name before potential customers. The refinement of lay-out and the quality of printing needed will depend on the product or service. The skilled tradesman offering a repair and maintenance service to local householders may be adequately served by a very simply produced leaflet. The new high-class delicatessen may require a professionally-produced sheet to create the right image. In both cases, however, the same rules apply – keep it simple, make clear the benefits available to the customers, and why they should use the service or buy the product.

Advertising This can sometimes be an effective way of getting the message across. For the small firm the more usual means are the daily or weekly local press, trade journals, free-issue advertising papers and the telephone (commercial) directory. However, it can be very expensive and there are often cheaper alternatives.

To help in finding the right publication for any particular business there are reference books in most local libraries – a well known one in the United Kingdom is *BRADS* (*British Rate and Data*). They carry an exhaustive list of publications including details of advertising rates, circulations and telephone numbers. Using these guides it is a straightforward matter to select several publications which appear to cover an adequate number of readers in the right sorts of trades or income groups in the right parts of the country. Inspection of back copies of these publications (usually available in larger libraries), or free 'voucher copies', often available on request from publishers, will then help to pin-point those which are most suitable. Finally, before the decision to place the advertisement is taken, the cost must be checked to assess whether the revenue likely to be generated warrants the expenditure.

The advertisement should be designed to:

Gain attention,
Arouse interest,
Be persuasive, and
Tell the reader what to do next.

To meet these demands it must be simple, relevant, well presented and contain just enough information to influence the reader to make an enquiry. It will probably be necessary to repeat the advertisement several times to re-inforce the message. It may also be necessary to publish it in different publications to make sure of reaching enough readers.

It is possible to use the services of advertising agencies to deal with these matters, but these bodies principally meet the needs of larger companies; and the costs involved may be too great for the small firm to bear. So the new venture usually has to do its own research and preparation. One source of help could be the advertising department of the local newspaper if that is the chosen medium. The staff are often prepared to give advice on the style, lay-out and position of the advertisement in the paper. Because advertising can be so expensive it is advisable to start on a moderate scale, monitor the results and only broaden the scope when it is reasonably certain that the results justify the expenditure.

Mail shots The postal service can be a very useful medium for sending persuasive messages to potential customers. If the earlier research has been successful the various directories used will have yielded a useful list of names and addresses.

Since the mail shot has to compete with other items received in the post it must draw attention to itself by being attractively presented. If it is to be read it must be clear and simple. All this means that a lot of thought is called for in the design and presentation.

A typical response rate from a mail shot is usually fairly low (in the order of 2–5 per cent) and so a large mailing will be necessary in order to elicit a reasonable number of replies. Various studies have shown, however, that the response rates can often be improved considerably by following certain guidelines:

Address mail shots to named individuals.
Type 'Private and Confidential' on the envelope.
If practicable have letters produced by a secretarial bureau possessing a word processor service rather than use a photocopier.
Keep it short and to the point.

Include photographs where possible.
Sign each letter individually.
Enclose a reply-paid card.

Brochures and catalogues Brochures and catalogues are usually prepared to provide information to a specific group of customers. When designing such literature, therefore, this group must be kept firmly in mind. There must be adeqate information – technical or otherwise – for the interested recipient to evaluate the goods or service, but the temptation to put too much in too small a space must be resisted – the result of doing this could be a product which appears unreadable and it may therefore not be read or only scanned cursorily.

The cost of producing this type of publicity material can be quite high, and prices charged by different printers can vary considerably. It is usually worth while getting several quotations. Costs will increase dramatically if more than one colour is used, photographs or other illustrations are included, or if the literature is to be bound or stapled. So, unless absolutely necessary, too many refinements should be avoided, especially during the initial period of setting up the business. Nevertheless, any publicity material which is produced must be professional and businesslike in appearance.

A routine for preparing literature of this type would consist of five stages:

(1) Formulate ideas,
(2) Draw up the rough form,
(3) Have the rough form refined and developed by the printer,
(4) Check the final form,
(5) Release for printing.

In formulating the ideas the following check-list is useful:

Why is the literature necessary?
Who is it aimed at?
What is to be described?
What information, technical or otherwise, will the recipient need?
Are pictures or diagrams needed?
Is colour essential to draw attention to the product or to clarify technical details?

Exhibitions and trade fairs Exhibition space can be very expensive, and this method of promotion is unlikely to be appropriate to any but a very small number of new firms. One advantage of exhibiting is that the product can be shown in association with other products appealing to the same market. Another advantage is that the product which incorporates advanced technology is placed in an environment to which trade buyers may be attracted from home and overseas. The exhibition itself may not generate a substantial number of orders, but it could well result in a useful number of enquiries to be followed up later. More appropriate to the small firm may be the local trade fair, which will cost less than the exhibition and attract from the locality buyers for specific products or services.

Editorial features The proprietor of the new shop, service business, or factory often overlooks a very effective and free means of getting the name of the firm better known – an article in the local daily or weekly newspaper. Local commercial radio stations now add to the scope for free publicity. Most editors are on the look-out for interesting pieces of news, and these can often be provided by the new firm. Naturally the item of news will not directly advertise the product or service, but the implications may be clear. For example the photographer who has just won a special prize for his work, the craftswoman whose textile products have been specially commended by some local society, the old, well-known building converted to a specialist restaurant, may all have news value.

In certain circumstances, for example when the product embodies unique technical features, it may be beneficial to produce a special paper for publication in trade or professional journals. As an alternative, the paper may be submitted to a meeting or conference of the appropriate body and thus command wide publicity.

Personal contact Whatever other means are used it is certain that very few businesses will make sales without personal contact between the seller and the buyer. The proprietor of the new firm will have to undertake this activity as well as managing all the other functions. In a well-balanced partnership it is likely that one partner will have some skills in selling and will undertake these duties. The firm making a product will probably feel the need at a later stage of growth to delegate the task of selling. Employing a salesman can be very expensive, and while it is unwise to quote any rules-of-thumb, it is worth bearing in mind that in many types of business a salesman has to generate extra annual sales amounting to perhaps five to ten times his annual salary and expenses. Alternatively it may be worth considering using an agent who would sell the product on commission.

If the role is filled by a partner or salesman it is essential that his activities are carefully controlled so that maximum value is gained from the time devoted to visits to potential customers. Every effort should be made to ensure that the person seen is the real decision maker. This is not necessarily the person who places the order—in a manufacturing company it might be the factory manager, the works engineer or the designer for example. Sales routes should be carefully planned so that as many calls as possible are made during a visit to a particular area. To make best use of time it is advisable to make appointments before calling, to enquire at each call if the contact can indicate any other possible customers in the area, and only make other, unplanned calls – in the jargon 'cold calls' – to fill in the gaps in the day.

The techniques of salesmanship are an entire subject in themselves and the person whose type of business depends largely on the skills of selling should study some of the many books written on the subject. In brief, however, the person hoping to succeed in selling will:

Know the product or service well.
Be well supplied with any samples or literature needed to inform the customer.
Have prepared in advance the main points of the presentation.
Be polite and buinesslike.
Understand the needs of customer.
Spell out the benefits clearly.
Ask questions to check the effect made on the potential buyer.
Anticipate, listen to, and answer the buyer's objections.
Ask for the order at the right moment.
Avoid criticising competitors directly.

Distribution

The next stage in the marketing process is to take steps to see that the goods or service reach the customer. To the retailer or provider of a service the word distribution may appear to be only of academic interest with its connotations of networks of retail outlets, wholesalers, road and rail links, and other features usually associated with large manufacturing concerns or merchants. But even the retailer has to consider whether or not to lay out the shop for self-service or personal service; whether to aim at the customer who wants a speedy transaction, or the customer who looks for advice and wishes to discuss the merits of the goods before buying; or even to offer a delivery service. Similarly, the hairdresser has the choice of dealing with clients on his own premises, or visiting them in their homes. The printer of high-class stationery for special events might find a useful outlet by working in conjunction with a local photographer.

The manufacturer who produces a product rather than offering a sub-contracting service must give serious thought to the means by which the goods are to be delivered from the factory gate and sold to the customer. Usually the choice is limited to selling to the customer either directly or through the trade. The main advantage of going through the trade is that the manufacturer has access to an established distribution system. The main disadvantages are that the profits will be reduced because the dealer has to allow a margin of profit, and also the manufacturer has little control over the selling operation. This can be a particular problem when the dealer also stocks competitors' products.

Some businesses may be able to distribute through a large manufacturer. For example, a firm making equipment for motor-cars or lorries might be able to arrange for the product to be quoted as an optional extra which can be fitted either at the factory or by dealers.

Selling directly to the customer may increase the manufacturer's profit margin. It also offers the advantage that control of the selling operation is much improved and single-minded commitment is assured. The opinions, complaints or favourable attitudes of customers can be assessed more quickly – an essential ingredient in developing the product and refining selling methods. On the other hand, initial costs are much higher because of the work involved in getting established with customers. Also the administrative tasks of delivering small orders and controlling credit are multiplied many times.

For many types of product it may be better to begin by going through the trade and switch to direct selling at a later date. If the product is technically very advanced it is probably better to consider direct selling. Otherwise the problem arises of training the dealer's sales team, the members of which may be less than enthusiastic about mastering complicated technical details.

In this chapter the various features of marketing the goods or services have been dealt with separately so that the many aspects can be studied in detail. It will, however, be obvious by now that they cannot, in practice, be isolated as they interact with each other. The choice of service or product is influenced by the type of customers most readily accessible. The type of product or service will influence the content of the message and the means of getting the message to the customer. The method of distribution chosen affects the amount of preliminary market research necessary before launching a product. The size and nature of the competition affects pricing policy and distribution methods. The number of ways in which these factors interact are many, and the lesson is clear: before taking decisions on any of these aspects the possible effects on all the other aspects must be thought out.

Summary

Before attempting to launch any business a large number of questions must be asked to establish that there is a market and that the business can capture an adequate share of it. When this is established the best means must be found of reaching that market with a message which simply but clearly states the special selling features of what is being offered. Finally, the most appropriate means of actually selling or distributing the product must be decided. Throughout the process the way in which the various aspects interact must be carefully thought out before action is taken.

Now we are ready to consider the problem of cash – how much is needed to launch the venture, and where it will come from – and this is the subject of the next chapter.

3 Finding the Cash

How Much Cash?

The new business needs cash for two purposes. First, to set up the enterprise, and then to finance the day-to-day operation of the business. This day-to-day requirement is usually termed *working capital*. In calculating initial requirements we must therefore establish how much cash is needed before trading can start, and then how much working capital will be required in the early days of trading before revenue begins to flow in. To these figures the proprietor will need to add an amount to cover personal needs – living expenses, mortgage repayments, etc. The total represents the capital which is required to launch the firm, and ensure its survival during the first months. However, the prudent person will realise that things might not go exactly as planned and will add a further sum to allow for any contingencies.

The calculation is best illustrated by looking at the expenditure to be incurred by a firm proposing to make timber products, working in rented premises (Fig. 3.1).

Sources of Cash

In Figure 3.1 cash is spent for one of two purposes: either it will finance the purchase of the items intended to remain permanently in the firm (plant and equipment), or it will be used to pay for materials, services and other items which are used in the day-to-day activities of the business. The first rule to observe when arranging funds for any business is that permanent items should, ideally, be financed by permanent or long-term funds. This means money which is permanently invested in the business or which does not have to be repaid for many years. The other items may – and in most cases should – be financed by funds which are repayable in the short or medium term.

Figure 3.1 *Expenditure of timber firm*

	£	£
1. *Acquisition of plant and equipment*		
Workshop:		
Paint sprayer	150	
Circular saw	500	
Bandsaw	600	
Router	150	
Driling machine	150	
Planer	600	
Spindle moulder	600	
Small tools	200	
Belt sander	150	
Lathe	300	
	3 400	
Office equipment	1 000	
Total		4 400
2. *Other expenses before trading*		
Professional expenses	600	
Advertising (to launch the product or service)	200	
Total		800
3. *Stock*		
Timber–quality A	1 000	
–quality B	600	
Other materials	200	
Total		1 800
Total initial capital		7 000
4. *Working capital for three months*		
Wages for 2 employees (including National Insurance contribution)	4 000	
Rent & rates	900	
Telephone	150	
Stationery and postage	200	
Heat, light, power	150	
Professional expenses	100	
Travel	150	
Advertising	150	
Total		5 800

Figure 3.1 *cont.*

5. *Salary for self to cover living expenses for 3 months*	2 000
6. *Contingency allowance*	1 000
Total capital required	15 800

Permanent or long-term funds

The first source of funds should be the owner(s) of the firm whether sole trader, partners, or shareholders in the limited company. When these funds are not adequate, the most usual course is to arrange a long-term loan with a private backer or a bank. This loan is unlikely to exceed the amount which the owners themselves are investing in the business. It is, in any case, unwise for the business to carry too large a loan, as the interest which has to be paid can prove a real burden, especially in the earlier years when profits may be hard to earn.

Usually the lender, especially if this is the bank, will expect to see a proposition from the borrower, so that he can make an assessment of the viability of the venture. The proposition will include details of the service or product, evidence of the type and anticipated number of customers, and a career history of the owner(s). Most lenders will also want to see included a forecast of the profit and loss account for the first year and a forecast of the end-of-year balance sheet. And they will certainly want to see a cash flow forecast. Figures 3.2, 3.3, 3.4 and 3.5 illustrate typical lay-outs of the forms which can be used to provide these details. (The three financial statements are discussed in some detail in later chapters.)

Even when the bank has approved the loan it is probable that some security will be required – usually a charge on property owned by the proprietor(s). The bank will also require regular reports on the progress of the business. Details of the services provided by the banks may be obtained from the managers of local branches of the High Street banks, or from the British Bankers Association, 10 Lombard St, London EC3V 9AP. Other sources of funds include:

Finance Houses Association Ltd
14 Queen Anne's Gate, London SW1H 9AG

Small Business Capital Fund
88 Baker Street, London W1M 1DC

Council for Small Industries in Rural Areas
35 Camp Road, Wimbledon Common, London SW19 4UP

In addition there are various schemes for helping to launch new firms, financed or supported by national or local government. Some schemes operate in conjunction with the High Street banks and the manager is probably the best source of information on these. For other schemes details are usually available at town halls, council offices, or the Small Firms Centres of the Department of Industry.

The most usual source of short-term cash is a bank overdraft. Once the manager is satisfied with the soundness of the proposals he will usually be prepared to accommodate these requirements by granting an overdraft facility. As with the bank loan he will want to see a cash flow forecast for the next year before agreeing to the facility, and may also require some personal guarantee. Not only is the overdraft the most common source of funds, it is also one of the least expensive, and for this reason many firms try to finance too much of their requirements by this means rather than by a loan. This is unwise, as any curtailment in overdraft facilities could place the business in jeopardy.

It may appear to the enthusiastic entrepreneur that banks and other financial institutions are too cautious in their lending policies. It must be remembered, however, that these organisations are in business to lend money in exchange for an adequate return and security, so they wish to be assured that the profits will be available to pay the interest. Furthermore, they do not like businesses to fail, even when the security is adequate to cover the loan, but prefer to be associated with enterprises with a reasonable chance of success. They are usually ready to help with sound advice both before the launch of the business and when it is in operation. There is seldom a shortage of cash for the well-conceived business being started by a competent person.

A word of advice to the person who is seeking funds for the first time may be in order at this stage. In order to get the best deal possible it is wise to shop around the different banks and compare the amounts they are prepared to lend, the interest rates charged, provisions for repayment, and the security demanded.

Figure 3.2 *Forecast profit and loss account for first year of trading*

	£	£
Sales revenue		45 000
Materials	15 000	
Wages	12 000	
Total direct expenses		27 000
Gross profit		18 000
Overhead expenses		
Salary	6 000	
Repairs & renewals	300	
Heat & light	600	
Rent & rates	3 250	
Telephone	600	
Stationery	850	
Travelling	600	
Professional services	1 000	
Advertising	900	
Depreciation	400	
Total		14 500
Surplus before interest charges		3 900

Figure 3.3 *Forecast balance sheet at end of first year*

Liabilities		*Assets*		
Capital	8 000	*Fixed assets*		
		Plant & equipment		4 000
Loan	4 000			
Undistributed profit	2 000			
Current liabilities:		*Current assets*		
Creditors	6 000	Debtors	6 000	
		Stock	9 500	
		Cash	500	
		Total		16 000
Total	20 000	*Total*		20 000

Figure 3.4 *Cash flow forecast*

	April	*May*	*June*	*July*	*December*	*January*	*February*
Cash in hand or at bank at start of month	8 000*	1 720	−2 870	−2 460			
Inflow of cash from customers	–	–	2 500	3 000			
Outflow of cash:							
Fixed assets	3 400	1 000	–	–			
Advertising	100	100	50	50			
Professional expenses	–	300	–	–			
Raw materials	900	900	–	500			
Wages & salaries	1 500	1 500	1 500	1 500			
Rent	170	170	170	170			
Rates	–	400	–	–			
Telephone	50	50	50	50			
Stationery	60	70	70	70			
Electrical	–	–	100	–			
Gas	–	–	50	–			
Travel	50	50	50	50			
Other expenses	50	50	50	50			
Total	6 280	4 590	2 090	2 440			
Cash increase (+) or decrease (−)	−6 280	−4 590	+410	+560			
Cash balance (+) or deficit (−)	+1 720	−2 870	−2 460	−1 900			

* Owner's investment

Figure 3.5 *Career history*

George Edward Robinson
54 Acacia Grove
Solihull
West Midlands B91 1HT
Tel: 021–744 4054

Date of Birth: 28 February 1939.

Education

1952–5	Bordesley Green Technical School–GCE English, Economics, History

Business education and training

1958	Executive Development Course–Small Business Centre, Aston University
1968	Work Study Course–John Evans & Partners
1962	Statistical Quality Control Course–Hall Green Technical College
1955–60	Engineering Apprenticeship–Rover Co. Ltd

Professional and academic qualifications

1974	Technician Engineer (Council of Engineering Institution)
1974	Member Institute of Quality Assurance
1970	Member Institute of Sales Managers

Career summary

March–June 1978	Autico (1972) Ltd Automotive components and mechanisms	*Quality Executive* Responsible to M.D. for total quality function including process control, vendor control, vetting company design, and customer liaison. Staff 55.
March 1976–. February 1978	Fenmagol Ltd Tractors & agricultural machinery	*Quality Assurance Specialist* Responsible to M.D. for planning, monitoring and implementing quality requirements for plants in Africa, Asia, Australasia and Middle East. Staff 30.
March 1973–February 1976	Afreco Ltd, Zambia	*Technical Manager Automotive* Responsible to M.D. of manufacturing division for establishing local manufacturing facilities for components for Fiat cars. Completed 3-year contract.
May 1971–February 1973	Fabrelec Co. Ltd Fabrications, pressings, fire pumps, electric vehicles	*Group Quality Manager* Responsible to M.D. for company quality vendor control, and customer liaison. Gained approval for company with I.F.V. and A.Q.D. Staff 25.

Figure 3.5 *cont*.

1964–71	Carducts Ltd Automotive com-	1. *Tool Investigation Engineer* 2. *Production Foreman* Machining section of 70 operators. 3. *Senior Night Production Foreman* Clutch division, machining and assembly. 350 operators.
1961–4	Prevescon Ltd Pressure vessels, hydraulic controls, heat exchangers, radiators	*Quality Control Engineer* Responsible to M.D. for vendor control procedures and production acceptance tests. Staff 5.
1955–61	Drimanco (1950) Ltd	1. *Engineering Apprentice* 2. *Assistant Tool Engineer*

4 Sole Trader, Partnership, Limited Company or Co-operative

Before starting to trade the owner(s) of the firm must decide on the legal form it will take. This is a matter on which the advice of the accountant and solicitor will be invaluable. The more usual legal forms of business are: Sole trader, partnership or limited liability company. A fourth type which, although not new, has become more popular in recent years, partly as a result of government encouragement, is the industrial or service co-operative. The characteristic features of these four forms are outlined below, together with the merits and demerits of each.

Sole Trader

This is the simplest form of business. Any person may set up as a sole trader and start trading with little legal formality, provided that any local and national authority regulations are observed. Information on local regulations are available at the offices of the local authority within whose area the business is situated. It is a advisable to check, when selecting premises, the specific regulations applicable to the type of business to be conducted there.

National legislation is dealt with in chapter 12. However, before starting to trade the potential owner should note that he is required by law to inform certain bodies that the business is to start operations. First, all owners must notify the local office of the Inland Revenue that the firm is starting to trade. Secondly, if the business is to employ any persons other than close relatives of the owner the Department of Employment must be notified as soon as the first employee is engaged. Thirdly, and, of special interest to the manufacturing business, is that before any power-driven machines are operated the local Health and Safety Inspector must be informed.

Subject to these restraints, the sole trader may start in business under his own name without any legal formalities. However, if the business is to use any name other than the surname of the owner then there are certain rules which have to be observed:

The individual's name and address must be stated in legible characters on all business letters, on written orders for goods and services, and on invoices.

The owner must display his name and address in any premises to which customers and suppliers have access, in a prominent position so that it may easily be read.

This form of business is probably the most appropriate for small retailing outlets or persons offering a personal service such as hairdressing, decorating or plumbing. In general it is a suitable form for the very small undertaking in which it is accepted that there is a very small non-insurable financial risk. The advantage of setting up as a sole trader is that there is a minimum of formality and the only cost involved will be the cost of any professional advice which the owner may decide to seek.

The disadvantage lies in the fact that there is no distinction in law between the owner and the business. The serious aspect of this is that the debts and obligations of the firm are regarded as those of the owner. Consequently, creditors may make claims on the personal estate of the owner for any debts owed to them by the firm. In the extreme case the failure of the firm could result in the bankruptcy of the owner.

Because the owner and the business are one and the same any profit made by the business belongs to the proprietor and is in consequence subject to income tax. This may be an advantage or a disadvantage depending on the level of profit expected.

Bearing in mind all these considerations the prudent owner will consult the accountant and solicitor before taking the decision to start business as a sole trader. The advice of the solicitor is especially important if the intention is to trade under the name other than that of the owner as there are certain restrictions on the use of certain words or names in the title of the firm.

It is possible of course, – and quite usual, – for a firm to start as a sole trader and later develop into a partnership or be incorporated as a limited liability company.

Partnership

When two or more persons carry on a business in common with a view to making profit, a partnership exists. There must be a minimum of two partners and, in most cases, a maximum of twenty.

The partnership is also subject to the requirements already outlined for the sole trader – notification of the tax inspector, the Department of Employment, and the Health and Safety Inspector. Similarly, if the name of the firm does not consist of the surnames of all partners then these names must appear on the stationery of the firm and be prominently displayed on the premises.

Although it is not a legal necessity, it is advisable to have a formal agreement between the partners drawn up by a solicitor, which defines the relationship between the partners and with third parties. If such an agreement is not drawn up it will be assumed in any subsequent legal actions that the provisions laid down in the Partnership Act 1890 will apply. (The legal position of a partnership is different in Scotland from that in the rest of the United Kingdom.) The minimum requirement for the contents of any agreement are:

- The name of the proposed partnership.
- The business address.
- The nature of the proposed business (what the business intends to provide as a service or as goods for sale).
- The names of those proposing to form the partnership.
- The date the partnership commenced.
- The duration of the partnership, if for a fixed period of time.
- The rights or otherwise of any partners to participate in the management of the partnership.
- Provision for the death, bankruptcy or retirement of partners and admitting new partners.
- Provisions and circumstances for the dissolution of the partnership and, in consequence, the partners' rights.
- Time to be devoted to the affairs of the partnership by each partner.
- Restrictions on the powers of any partner to make a contract or incur any liability on behalf of the partnership.
- Details of the capital contribution from each partner and provisions for further injections of capital.
- How the profits and loss shall be divided, if not in proportion to the capital contributions.
- Salary entitlement for acting in the partnership.

How drawings (withdrawal of cash or kind) shall be made from the business, and whether these shall be the subject of 'Current' Accounts rather than Capital Accounts.
Arrangements for the keeping of proper books of account.
Provision for arbitration on matters giving rise to dispute.

It must be reiterated that, whatever agreement is made between the partners themselves, *all* partners are liable in law without limit to third parties for the debts and other obligations of the partnership.

The partnership form of organisation has the advantage of simplicity similar to that applying to the sole trader. It also has the same disadvantage – the firm is not distinguished in law from the partners forming the firm. The partners jointly and severally are responsible for meeting the debts and other obligations of the firm to third parties.

The profits of the partnership will be divided between the partners in accordance with any agreement made between them and thus will be subject to tax at the individual partner's rate of income tax.

This form of business is generally suitable for the provision of professional and personal services on a larger scale than can be offered by a sole trader.

Great care should be exercised in the choice of partners. Perhaps the two most important features are that the personal objectives of the partners are not incompatible with the needs of the business, and that the personalities of the individuals are acceptable to each other. Many firms have failed because these features were lacking even when the abilities and resources of the partners were otherwise perfectly adequate. Among other matters to be considered are the skills required in the firm and how these can be provided by the partners – the practical man may feel the need for a partner with business skills; the designer may need a partner skilled in getting things made. In general, the skills should be complementary rather than similar. And the personal financial resources of the individual partners must also be taken into account if a well-balanced partnership is to be established.

Limited Liability Company

The principal disadvantage of the sole trader or the partnership lies in the fact that the owner(s) carry an unlimited liability for the debts and obligations of the business. This can be overcome by forming a limited liability company. This is a company registered under the

Companies Act 1948–81 and the legal requirements and constraints are very much stricter than for sole traders or partnerships. When a firm is incorporated as a limited liability company it thereby assumes an entirely separate legal personality. It is independent of its owners, whose liability for the debts of the company is limited to the investment they have agreed to make by buying shares in the company.

There are two kinds of limited company – the public company (denoted by the initials plc) and the private company. The private company is not allowed to offer its shares to the public, and this is the type of company which is appropriate to the small business. This book deals only with private companies.

The private limited company must have at least two members, but there is no statutory maximum. In order for the business to be incorporated it has to be approved and registered for England and Wales by:

Registrar of Companies,
Companies Registration Office,
Crown Way, Maindy, Cardiff CF4 3UZ.

for Scotland:

Companies Registration Office,
Exchequer Chambers,
102 George Street, Edinburgh EH2 3DJ.

A set of documents must be filed with the Registrar, and it is advisable when preparing these to seek the help of the solicitor or other specialist experienced in the formation of companies. The two chief documents required are:

(1) *The Memorandum of Association* which sets out the –
name of the company,
country in which the registered office is situated,
objects for which the company is established,
limitation of the liability of its members,
share capital of the company, numbers and value of each class of share,
association clause in which the subscribers declare that they desire to be formed into a company, and give an undertakiang to take up the shares shown opposite their names.

Each subscriber is required to sign the Memorandum and to have the signature witnessed.

(2) *The Articles of Association*
This provides detailed regulations for the internal management of the company's affairs. A company may, if it wishes, adopt the Articles set down in Table A of Schedule I of the Companies Act 1948–81. If it is likely that these will not meet the needs of the company completely, it may either exclude Table A completely and file its own articles; or exclude, as appropriate, certain provisions and substitute its own. The provisions in Table A relate to such matters as share capital and variation of right, transfers of share, lien, general meetings and proceedings at general meetings.

There are three other documents which have to be filed at the same time:

(1) A statement giving particulars of the first directors and company secretary.
(2) A declaration that the requirements of the Companies Act with regard to registraton have been complied with.
(3) A statement of the capital of the company.

The limited company is usually the most suitable form of organisation for the larger small firm, especially in manufacturing industry, where the risks of financial loss might be great. The obvious advantage is that the owners' financial commitment is limited to their shareholding in the company. This may prove to be illusory however, particularly in the early days of the venture, if the business takes credit from suppliers or relies on loans to finance its operations. Such persons may require personal guarantees for the amount of credit or loan. Frequently the only security which can be offered is the owners' private property, so that the private fortune of the owners is at risk. The personal estate of the owner can also be at risk if the business fails and it can be shown that the failure was due to a breach of his duties as a director.

The main disadvantages of setting up as a limited company are first, that it may involve long and fairly expensive preparatory legal work, and secondly, that when formed the company has to make annual returns to the Registrar.

Because the company is a separate body, existing in its own right, any profit made is subject to corporation tax which is at a different rate from the personal tax rates of the owners. This may or may not be an advantage to the owners, depending on the level of profits of the company and the personal circumstances of the owners.

Industrial or Service Co-operative

This form of organisation provides an alternative for persons who wish to enjoy the benefit of limited liability but do not wish to be incorporated under the Companies Act. The legal status of a co-operative is defined in the Industrial and Provident Societies Act (I and PS Act). The concept behind the co-operative venture is that the members should participate in running the business for the mutual benefit of the members or for the community. The Act, while not specifically defining a co-operative, states that the term may not be applied to 'a society which carries on, or intends to carry on business with the object of making profits mainly for the payment of interest, dividends or bonuses on money invested or deposited with or lent to the society or any other person'.

A co-operative must be registered with the Registrar of Friendly Societies and must satisfy the following conditions:

The benefits enjoyed by the co-operators depend on their participation in the venture and not on the amount of their individual investments.

There is no deliberate intention to limit admission to membership in order to increase the value of existing member holdings.

Control is on the principle of one person, one vote.

This form of organisation is applicable to any small-scale manufacturing or service business. However, the Act lays down strict rules for distribution of any profits that may be made, and any interest which may be paid on loans. The person who wishes to build up a profitable business for the purpose of personal gain would therefore be wise to set up the business in one of the other forms described.

In 1978 the government set up the Co-operative Development Agency (CDA) to promote this type of co-operation. Other bodies have also developed during recent years for the same purpose. Notable among these are: The Industrial Common Ownership Movement (ICOM), The Co-operative Union Limited (CUL) and Job Ownership Limited (JOL). Persons intending to set up a co-operative are well advised to get in touch with these bodies (addresses are given below) as they can make the task of registration much easier for the inexperienced person. For example, ICOM has produced a set of model rules which have been approved by the Registrar. When a group joins ICOM as an associate member not only may it use these rules but it obtains a very substantial reduction in the registration fee. In 1982 this fee was £179, reduced to £84 for

ICOM members. There is a fee payable on joining ICOM, which also charges a fee for handling applications on behalf of members. However, at £25 and £20 respectively these are small sums compared with legal and other fees involved when a limited company is set up.

Addresses:
CDA, 20 Albert Embankment, London SW1 7TJ
ICOM, Beechwood College, Elmete Lane, Roundhay, Leeds LS8 2LQ
CUL, The General Secretary, Co-operative Union Ltd Holyoake House, Hanover Street, Manchester M60 OAS
JOL, 42 Hanway Street, London W1P 9DE.

To complete this chapter a note on value added tax is appropriate. All businesses having a sales turnover of more than a certain value (fixed from time to time by the Chancellor of the Exchequer and currently £17,000 per annum) must register for VAT with the Customs and Excise. This figure is so low that it will be exceeded by practically all partnerships, limited companies, and co-operatives, so that exemption from VAT will apply, in the main, to those sole traders who provide a personal service. However, even businesses with a sales turnover below the limit may elect to register and in some cases it might be advisable to do so. This applies when the majority of transactions are with customers who are registered for VAT, and it may be advisable to discuss this matter with the accountant when the business is being formed. The Customs and Excise publish a large number of free booklets dealing with the scope of VAT and its application to various types of trade. The local telephone directory will give the address and telephone number of the local office of HM Customs and Excise.

5 Keeping the Books

Many a person has started out in business hopefully and energetically with all the dedication and perseverance so necessary to success; but the firm has failed to realise its full potential. In a large number of cases, the cause of failure has been a lack of necessary control in one or more functions of the business. Prominent among these, in the experience of the authors, has been the lack of control over financial matters. This and subsequent chapters deal with this aspect of running the business, and the purpose of these chapters is to indicate to the potential owner how the financial information available may be used to keep the business under control.

Most people now thinking of starting their own business will probably have been working as employees, possibly in medium or large companies. Very few – except those who have been employed in the accounting department – will have needed to know anything about the process of keeping accounts. Even managers and directors, who may have been presented with financial results by their accountants, will probably not be familiar with the method of their preparation. They might understand the implications of the figures, but the mechanics of producing them has not been their concern.

In running one's own business this deficiency must be remedied. Almost certainly, in the early days the owner will have to keep the records necessary to provide financial information, or at least supervise someone else's doing so. We do not attempt in this book to teach book-keeping; rather, we attempt to help the potential owner to decide what records should be kept if the business is to be kept under control. When the owner has decided what information is required, it is the function of the accountant to advise on the exact form of the books which must be kept. In an earlier chapter we emphasised the importance of appointing an accountant who will not only audit the books but will also help in preparing the financial information in a way which helps the owner to control the business effectively.

Because the results of the activities of any business are eventually measured in financial terms, the one function which is common to all is the accounting function. In the one-man business this function will be the task of the owner; the large company will employ a department of specialists. But the purpose of the function is the same – to assemble information, and express it in financial terms. The process is in essence the same: to collect the information, record it in suitable books of account, prepare statements showing the profit or loss and (in enlightened businesses), present the information in a manner which helps the owner to control the business.

This chapter deals with the tasks involved in collecting and recording the transactions of the company. Later chapters cover the other activities of the accounting function.

Basic Documents

It is an essential initial step to ensure that the business has sufficient and adequate documentation to provide evidence that each transaction has taken place and to provide the basis of a system of book-keeping which in turn provides information for the production of the financial statements and control of the business. These documents and records need not be elaborate nor complex, but they must be appropriate to the needs of the business and to the discharge of certain obligations imposed by the state. (The obligations which entail keeping accurate accounts and the preparation of annual accounts will be dealt with in some detail in later chapters.)

A typical set of essential documents is described below:

Purchase Orders – all businesses have to buy goods or services from time to time. From the start of operations it is a good practice to insist that the orders for these items are prepared on a specially designed form, signed by the owner or an appointed deputy. This is not to say that orders may not be given over the telephone, but any such order should be confirmed on the proper form and a copy retained. The order form should show:

the name and address of the firm,
the name and address of the supplier to whom the order is being given,
the date,
a description of the items ordered,
the quantities,
the price of each item,

when delivery is required, and
any other specific instructions to the supplier.

An example of a purchase order is shown in Figure 5.1.

Goods Received Record – when the goods which have been ordered are delivered it is essential that there should be a procedure for receiving them and recording their arrival. The document used may be a specially printed form for each delivery, or it may be a book in which all deliveries are recorded. The essential information to be recorded on the form or in the book is:

the date of the delivery,
the supplier's name,
a short description of the goods,
the quantity, and
the carrier.

It is important that before goods are put into stock they are inspected to ensure, as far as is possible, that they meet the specification, and are not damaged or sub-standard in any way; and it is particularly important to check that the quantity and specification of goods received agree with the details on the purchase order. If this is not done, they may be taken into stock and the defects or shortages not noticed until they are taken from stock for use or re-sale, resulting in serious delays whilst defective goods are returned, and replacements obtained. Even worse, the supplier might refuse to accept liability if a long time has elapsed since the goods were delivered. A typical goods received list is illustrated in Figure 5.2.

Stock Cards/Stock Book – in order that control over stock can be maintained it is important that a simple record is kept. The record may be kept on specially designed cards, one card per item of stock, or it may be kept in a stock book. This second method is not usually desirable as it tends to be less convenient in use, especially when several people wish to refer to it at the same time. It may, however, be perfectly satisfactory for the one-man, or very small, business. Essentially, only three columns are needed: goods received, goods issued, and balance in stock.

Many systems in use provide for extra information – for example to include details of goods on order, and goods allocated to customers' orders which are not yet due on delivery. This information allows the person keeping the record to check how much stock is not already reserved for special orders and therefore which of this may be used or sold. The same type of document can be used for both the

Figure 5.1 *Purchase order*

UNIMANCO
The Universal Manufacturing
Company Limited

200 Forest Industrial Park
Hogarth Way
West Midlands B6 4SY
Telephone: 021–359 4647

Order no.	
Date	
Important:	To ensure minimum delay in settlement our order no. must be quoted on all documents.

Description	*Quantity*	*Unit*	*Price*

Delivery required by:

Delivery instructions:

Value of order (excl. VAT)

For and on behalf of

PURCHASE ORDER

Registration No: 1122695 England

VAT no. 377:3370:31

Figure 5.2 *Goods received list*

DAILY STORES RECEIVED LIST *No.:*

Date:

Supplier	*Advice note no.*	*Carrier*	*Description*	*Quantity*

stock of raw materials and components used in manufacture or for finished goods. An example of this type of card is illustrated in Figure 5.3.

Goods Despatch/Advice Note – Any commercial enterprise exists by selling goods or services to customers and receiving payment for them. It is therefore essential to have some evidence that the firm has despatched the goods or completed the service in accordance with the customers' orders. When the transaction requires the despatch of goods a common practice is to send with the goods two notes, usually identical except for title – the first entitled a contents note, the second a despatch note. Frequently, customers are asked to sign the despatch note and return it to the supplier, via the carrier, while the contents note remains with the customer. Alternatively, an advice note may be sent to the customer by post. One advantage of sending the note separately is that should the goods not arrive for any reason, the customer is able to report the non-arrival promptly. See Figure 5.4 for the lay-out of the note.

Sales Invoice – As soon as the goods have been despatched or the service completed a sales invoice must be sent to the customer. It is important that there is no delay in sending off this document, as any delays here will mean that payment will be delayed, and the firm's cash flow affected. The invoice should be prepared in duplicate,

Figure 5.3 *Stock card*

Stock record card *Card no.* *Description* *Minimum stock* *Maximum stock*

Receipts			Issues			Balance	On order			Allocation			Free stock
Date	Order no.	Quantity	Date	Issue note no.	Quantity		Date	Order no.	Quantity	Date	Works order no.	Quantity	

Figure 5.4 *Advice note*

UNIMANCO
The Universal Manufacturing
Company Limited

200 Forrest Industrial Park
Hogarth Way
West Midlands B6 4SY

Telephone: 021–123 4567

Date

Advice note no.

Please advise if delivery is not
received within 14 days

Description	*Quantity*	*Unit*

Delivery address:

Carrier:

Received by:

ADVICE NOTE

Registration No: 1122695 England VAT no. 377:3370:31

using the information in the despatch note as the basis for preparation. The information to be included is:

the name and address of the business,
the customer's name and address,
number and date of the invoice,
payment terms and entitlement to settlement discounts,
quantity and description of the goods/service supplied,
price of each item invoiced,
total value of all items on the invoice.

If the firm is registered for VAT it is a legal requirement that the VAT registration number and VAT amount are also included. A specimen sales invoice is illustrated in Figure 5.5.

In the retailing business most customers pay at the time of making the purchase so that there is no need for a sales invoice. Instead the retailer should have a till which incorporates keys for the simple classification of goods, and tally rolls on which sales are automatically recorded. However, many retailers may find it desirable to issue a receipt to the customer as proof of purchase. This provides useful evidence when goods are returned as faulty, or when charges of shop lifting are being preferred, and may be printed automatically by certain types of till.

Time Sheets/Time Book – if the business employs people it is desirable that a record of the hours worked by each person is maintained. In some firms it may be that a simple record of time-on and time-off is all that is required to be used as the basis for preparing the pay roll. In other firms a more detailed record is kept of the hours spent by each employee on each job as an aid to establishing the costs of jobs, and providing guidance for estimates in the future. When this extra information is required it is usual to complete one time sheet per employee on a form similar to that in Figure 5.6. It may be filled in by the person concerned, by a supervisor, or by the owner. There are more complicated systems involving the use of special clock cards and clocking machines, but these are unnecessary in the majority of small firms.

Petty Cash Voucher – this document is used when the business makes purchases of small value from local traders, or when it is necessary to reimburse persons for travelling or other out-of-pocket expenses incurred on behalf of the business. It is good practice to insist right from the beginning that all such expenditure is recorded on a petty cash voucher. It is easier to instil this good habit at the start than later on, when people may have become accustomed to

Figure 5.5 *Sales invoice*

UNIMANCO The Universal Manufacturing Company Limited	200 Forrest Industrial Park Hogarth Way West Midlands B6 4SY Telephone: 021–359 4646

	Invoice no. Date Advice note no. Settlement terms	Net cash 30 days from date of invoice

Description	*Quantity*	*Unit*	*Price*	*Amount*
Delivery address		Total VAT 15%		

Registration no: 1122695 England VAT no. 377:3370:3

SALES INVOICE

Figure 5.6 *Time sheet*

Week ending .... *Name.........*

Day	*Job no.*	*On*	*Off*	*Hours*		*Remarks*

dealing with petty cash rather more casually. A sample voucher is illustrated in Figure 5.7.

As the business develops, the owner will probably need other documents. It is important before introducing new paperwork systems to review the existing documents and procedures to see if they can be modified to meet the new need. If this is not done the number of documents in the business can increase to a surprisingly large number involving much unnecessary administrative work.

All document sent from the business should have a professional, business like appearance. Customers, suppliers and others who receive these documents from the firm may make judgements based on them which could affect their opinions of the firm, and whether they enter into a business relationship.

Basic Records

The information on the separate basic documents should now be assembled in a series of books, referred to by accountants as *books of original entry*. These are easy to use and readily understood, so the task of making entries should present no difficulty. There are five main books:

Purchases daybook,
Sales daybook,
Cash book (including the petty cash book),
Wages book (pay roll), and
Journal.

Figure 5.7 *Petty cash voucher*

Name		*Mileage allowance*		*Engine cc*	*Petrol* VAT *p/mile*		*Expense claim form*				*Sheet no.*
Date	*Details*	*Miles*	*Total amount*	*Remarks*	VAT	*Net total*	*Code*	*Analysis*			
Received				Date							

Note: (a) Items to be entered separately.
(b) Receipts/vouchers to be attached.

Purchases daybook

As the name suggests all invoices submitted by suppliers of goods or services are recorded in this book. It is also used to record credit notes received from the supplier for goods returned to them because they are defective or not to specification. As soon as the purchase invoice is received it should be checked against the purchase order. Suppliers can make mistakes so it is important to ensure that the prices and quantities are correctly stated, and that the calculations have been made accurately. It is not usual to enter each invoice individually as it is received. Depending on the number of invoices received, the daybook may be written up daily or weekly. Before making the entries it is good practice to marshal all the invoices in alphabetical order. When this is done, all the invoices from each individual supplier can be easily assembled and then entered at the same time. It is advisable at this stage to number all the invoices sequentially. This makes identification easier at subsequent stages in the book-keeping process; it is better to do this than to attempt to identify them by suppliers' own reference numbers which will, of course, not be in a sequencc suitable for use by their customers.

The purchases daybook should be designed so that the separate items are entered in such a way that subsequent analysis can be made under certain defined headings of the amounts of expenditure incurred. For example, the owner of the business may wish (or be advised by the accountant) to classify purchases under such headings as: materials (this may be one heading, or several to segregate different types of material), tools, stationery, electricity and gas, etc.

The analysis should also be extended to separate VAT from the purchase price. This will make much easier the task of completing VAT returns. Many proprietors of small firms appear to find the completion of these VAT forms a heavy burden, but if the purchases daybook is kept in this way the difficulties will be much reduced. When this type of analysis is carried out at this stage it not only provides information which is valuable to the owner in controlling the financial affairs of the business, but it can also result in reduced audit fees because the auditor's work will be made easier.

A sample page from a typical daybook is illustrated in Figure 5.8. This shows how the book can be laid out and how the information for analysis is recorded at the same time as the entry is made.

At the close of each month, or any other trading period the owner may have selected, each column should be added up and cross-balanced.

Figure 5.8 *Purchase daybook*

Page no: Month – *February*

Invoice	*Supplier*	*Folio*	*Invoice amount* £	*VAT* £	*STD Rate* £	*Zero Rate* £	*Exempt* £	*Materials Y* £	*Materials Z* £	*Heat & Light* £	*Rent* £	*Stationery* £
101	Electricity Board		150.00			150.00				150.00		
102	J.M. Stationers Ltd		34.50	4.50	30.00							30.00
103	J. Banyard Ltd		86.25	11.25	75.00			75.00				
104	J. Banyard Ltd		115.00	15.00	100.00			100.00				
105	J. Banyard Ltd		28.75	3.72	25.00				25.00			
106	S. Winters		100.00			100.00					100.00	
107	Post office		46.00	2.70	18.00	25.30						
	Total		4546.00	3540.00	531.00	475.00	–	700.00	350.00	240.00	100.00	120.00
			A	(1)	(2)	(3)	(4)	(5)	(6)	(7)	(8)	(9)

Columns 1, 2, 3 and 4 should equal the total in Column A. Columns 5, 6, 7, 8, 9 etc. plus Column 1 should also equal the Column A total. In this way confidence is gained as to the arithmetical accuracy of the records.

Sales daybook

The general arrangement of this book follows that of the purchases daybook, except that where the purchases daybook analyses entries by type of expenditure, the analysis columns in the sales daybook correspond to the different ranges of goods or services the business offers to its customers.

The reason for this analysis is that it enables the owner from time to time to make an assessment of the volume of business attributable to the different products or services offered to customers. This is useful information when decisions have to be taken on future policy concerning ranges of product or services to be offered. Figure 5.9 shows a typical lay-out for this method of analysis.

Sometimes the proprietor may wish to assess the volume of business generated by certain types of customer, or in certain regions of the country. When this is so the columns would be headed appropriately and the analysis made in the same way.

This record is prepared from the retained copies of the sales invoices. Entries should be made at least weekly. All the invoices which have been prepared since the date of the last entry should be marshalled and entered in number sequence in the same manner as for purchase invoices.

The cash book

This is a very simple but essential book to maintain. Every business will from time to time receive payments for the goods/services it has sold and make payments to suppliers for the goods/service it has purchased, and for wages and petty cash items, etc. A suggested ruling is shown in Figure 5.10(a). The process is relatively straightforward. All cheques, postal orders/bank notes received daily are entered on the left-hand (receipts) side:

Column 1 – the date of the receipt of the payment.
Column 2 – the name of the customer or other source of payment.
Column 3 – this entry is made later, at the time the customer's account is credited.
Column 4 – discounts allowed.
Column 5 – the value of the cheque.
Column 6 – the total value of cheques banked.

Figure 5.9 *Sales daybook*

Page no. 2 *Month – February*

Invoice no.	*Customer*	*Folio*	*Invoice amount*	*VAT*	*STD rate*	*Zero rate*	*Exempt*	*Product 1*	*Product 2*	*Product 3*	*Etc.*	*Carriage charged*
124	John Smith		115.00	15.00	100	–	–	50	50	–	–	–

Figure 5.10(a) *Cash Book*

DR (Receipts)												*(Payments) CR*
Date	*Account*	*Folio*	*Discount*	*Sales ledger*	*Bank*	*Date*	*Cheque no*	*Account*	*Folio*	*Discount*	*Wages & other*	*Purchase ledger*
5 May	J. Smith		–	115	–							
(1)	(2)	(3)	(4)	(5)	(6)	(7)	(8)	(9)	(10)	(11)	(12)	(13)

When the total of the amount received has been entered in the bank column, the bank paying in slip is prepared and the cheque/cash banked intact. It is important that any bank notes received are not used to meet petty cash or other expenses. Unless this rule is followed it will be difficult at a later stage to reconcile bank statements with the receipts from the various transactions. Apart from making the auditor's work more difficult, this could give rise to the opportunity for fraud.

The entries on the right-hand side represent all payments made by the firm to suppliers, employees or other recipients. The entries may be made from the cheque book stubs. These should always be completed after preparing the cheques, but before detaching them from the cheque book. The details to be entered on this side of the cash book are:

Column 7 – date of payment.
Column 8 – the last three digits of the cheque number.
Column 9 – the name of the payee.
Column 10 – this entry is made later at the time of payee's account is debited.
Column 11 – any discounts taken.
Column 12 – amount drawn from the bank for wages or petty cash.
Column 13 – amount of the cheque sent to the supplier.

At the close of each period the cash book columns should be added up and the owner will readily see whether the cash receipts exceeded the payments, or vice versa. From time to time the bank will send a bank statement showing a balance which may or may not agree with the balance shown in the cash book. It is therefore necessary to reconcile the two balances as shown below.

This should be done each time a bank statement is received so that the owner may be reasonable assured of the accuracy of the records of cash flowing in and out of the business. If the strict discipline advocated earlier in the chapter is followed and if all entries have been regularly and conscientiously made there should be little difficulty in affecting this reconciliation.

The petty cash book

The petty cash book is a subsidiary of the main cash book and is used to obviate the need to record numerous small value transactions in the main cash book. The two sources of the entries are the amount

Balance per bank statement at (date)
add amounts banked but not yet credited by bank:

(Details)

less cheques paid but not yet presented to bank:

(Details)

Balance per cash book folio

drawn from the bank for petty cash purposes, and the petty cash vouchers which show the purposes for which the cash has been used. Figure 5.10(b) shows a page from a typical petty cash book.

The first three columns show the date, the cash book reference number and the amount drawn from the bank for petty cash. The other columns should be self-explanatory. It will be noted that, in a similar manner to the purchases daybook, provision is made for recording VAT, and for analysing expenditure into the selected categories.

This book should be balanced weekly. If for any reason this is not practicable the interval should certainly not exceed one month. A simple statement will then show:

	£
Amounts drawn from bank	
Total of petty cash vouchers	
Balance of cash in hand	

It is important that absolute discipline is maintained in the control of the petty cash system. Carelessness can lead to difficulty when accounts have to be audited, and can also encourage misuse of funds.

Figure 5.10(b) *Petty cash book*

Page no. 2 *Month – February*

Date	*CB Fo*	*Amount £*	*Voucher no.*	*Description*	*Fo*	*Amount £*	*VAT £*	*STD £*	*Zero £*	*Exempt*	*Petrol*	*Postage*	*Etc.*
6.2.82	22	50.00	81	Petrol		16.00	2.09	13.91			13.91		
			82	Stamps (etc.)		3.10			3.10			3.10	

Figure 5.11 *Pay Record**

Address ______________________ Tax district ______________________

______________________ Tax reference No. ______________________

Date of Birth __________ Date started __________ Date left __________ Occupation __________

EARNINGS								
DATE	BASIC	A	B	C				

INCOME TAX	
DATE/WK. NO	TAX CODE

◀ If amended cross out previous code.

This box may be used to record the National insurance Table Letter in use. Enter in pencil in case of change.

Wk No. / Mth No.	DATE	EARNINGS BASIC	A	B	C STATUT SICK PAY	GROSS PAY THIS WEEK/ MONTH	SUPERANN CONTRIBN UNDER NET PAY SCHEME	GROSS PAY LESS SUPERANN CONTRIBN	CUMULATIVE TOTALS TOTAL PAY TO DATE	TOTAL TAX FREE PAY TO DATE	TOTAL TAXABLE PAY TO DATE	TOTAL INCOME DUE DA
1 — 27 / 1												
28 / 2												
2 — 29 / 3												
30 / 4												
3 — 31 / 5												
32 / 6												
4 — 33 / 7												
34 / 8												
5 — 35 / 9												
36 / 10												
6 — 37 / 11												
38 / 12												
7 — 39 / 13												
40 / 14												
8 — 41 / 15												
42 / 16												
9 — 43 / 17												
44 / 18												
10 — 45 / 19												
46 / 20												
11 — 47 / 21												
48 / 22												
12 — 49 / 23												
50 / 24												
13 — 51 / 25												
52 / 26												
14												

◀ PREVIOUS EMPLOYMENT(S) ▶

◀ THIS EMPLOYMENT (MARK REFUNDS 'R') ▶

* By permission of Moore Paragon UK Ltd

NI CONTN TABLE LETTER —

NATIONAL INSURANCE NO.

Surname

First 2 Forenames

Dept. Check No.

DEDUCTIONS			

The amount in this column is for information only. For Deduction purposes it is already included in "Employees Nat. Ins. Contributions".

NI CONTN TABLE LETTER	TOTAL OF EMPL'ERS NAT. INS. CONTRIB'NS	Deductions EMPEES NAT. INS. CONTRIB'NS	EMPEES NAT. INS. AT "CONTRACTED OUT" RATE	DEDUCTIONS INCOME TAX Refund Mark 'R'	1	2	3	TOTAL DEDUCTIONS	NET PAY	NON-TAXABLE ALLOWANCES	AMOUNT PAYABLE

N.I. TABLE LETTER & TOTALS

Enter letter identifying Contribution Table used when making first entry on Card and on change of Table. Enter separate Contribution Totals for each Table used. Make the entries in the Table Letter and Total boxes on the side containing the last weekly entry.

Pay records

These records may also be regarded as a subsidiary of the main cash book. The prime source of information is the time book or time sheets. Because of the statutory obligations imposed on the business, certain practices must be observed, particularly:

An itemised pay slip must be given to each employee showing gross pay, deductions and the net amount payable.
Income tax and National Insurance contributions must be deducted at source and properly accounted for.

A pay record giving the following information should be kept for every individual:

Name and address
Social security number
Income tax number
Rate of pay
Pension deductions
Any other deductions authorised by the employee
Detailed record of payments actually made weekly (or monthly) comprising:
  Gross pay made up from – basic pay
    overtime premiums
    bonuses, etc.
  Less pre-tax pension contributions
  Total pay this week (or month)
  Total pay to date
  Tax-free pay to date (from Tax Table A*)
  Taxable pay to date
  Tax due to date (from Tax Table B*)
  Tax paid to date
  Tax due on earnings for this pay period
  National Insurance contributions this period
  Other authorised deductions this period
  Net pay this week (or month)
Employer's share of National Insurance contributions
* These are provided by the Department of Inland Revenue.

There are several proprietary systems on the market which meet these requirements and thus the need to develop a special system can be avoided. A section of a typical pay roll is illustrated in Figure 5.11. Many systems make provision for the pay-slip to be made out at the same time as the pay roll. These systems produce an original and a copy, one line per employee. The copy is perforated so that when the pay roll has been prepared each employee's slip can be torn from the copy, leaving the original as the firm's record.

The Journal

The use of this book will be more easily understood when the description of the book-keeping process has been read (See pp. 74–79). It must be mentioned here to complete the list of books of original entry The main purpose of the book is to simplify the correction of errors which may have been made in the various ledgers. It is also used to adjust the amount to be paid to a supplier who may also be a customer who owes money to the firm. In this instance the amount owed can be offset against amounts owing and the balance settled by cheque. Another purpose is to record the depreciation of the assets of the business, though this latter matter will probably be attended to by the accountant when preparing final accounts, rather than by the manager or owner of the business.

A specimen entry in the Journal is illustrated in Figure 5.12.

Figure 5.12 *Journal*

Date	*Entry*	*fo*	*DR*	*CR*
6.2.82	John Smith		100.00	
	Joseph Smith			100.00
	Being the correction of the posting of Invoice 123, 12.1.82			

All the records described in this chapter should be maintained by the business as part of the normal process of business administration. At this stage it may be useful to summarise them:

Source of Information	
Sales invoice Sales credit notes	Sales daybook
Purchase invoices Purchase credit notes	Purchases daybook
Cash receipts Cash payments Petty cash vouchers, via petty cash book Wages and salaries, via wages book	Cash book
All documents and ledgers	Journal

The book-keeping process

We have now established the sources of information from which the accounts of the business are to be compiled, and have transferred this information into the books of original entry. The next step is to set up a system of books referred to in accountancy terms as *Books of Account*.

This system can be graphically depicted thus:

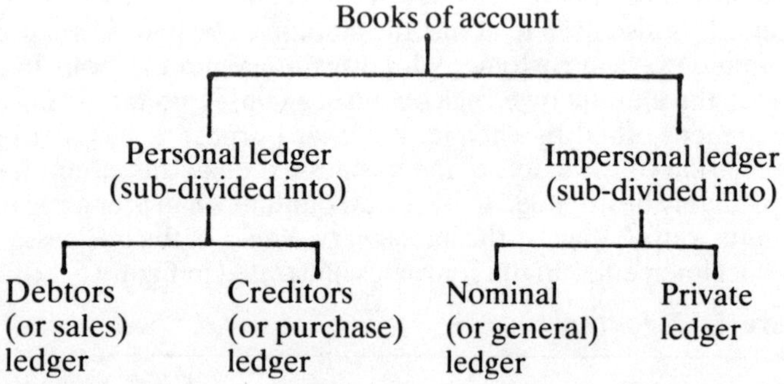

The personal ledger With the exception of some retail shops, most firms, and certainly practically all manufacturers, do business on credit terms. When they buy materials, goods or services they are given credit, which means they are given time to pay in accordance with the terms stipulated by the supplier. When they sell goods or services they in turn give credit to their customers. All such transactions are recorded, via the daybooks, in the personal ledger. This ledger may be a bound book, in which case one or more pages will be allocated to each individual supplier and each individual customer. In recent years the bound book has given way to loose-leaf systems. These offer the advantage that new pages may be added to the ledger when accounts are opened for new customers or new suppliers without disturbing the alphabetical sequence. The principle remains the same. Each customer and each supplying firm has its separate sheet or card on which the credit transactions with the firm are recorded.

It is usually convenient to sub-divide this ledger into two sections.

One part, dealing only with the customers' personal accounts, is termed the debtors (or sales) ledger. The other part, dealing only with the suppliers' personal accounts, is termed the creditors (or purchase) ledger.

It will be seen therefore that an individual person or company could have an account in both the debtors ledger and the creditors ledger. (See notes above on the use of the Journal.)

*The impersonal ledger*Unlike the personal ledger which contains details of transactions between the business and individuals or other firms, the impersonal ledger is concerned with the nature of goods and services which are sold or bought. The accounts with which the owner of the small firm will be mainly concerned are those dealing with the revenue from sales, and the costs incurred in the day-to-day running of the business. For this reason it is convenient to divide the impersonal ledger into two separate ledgers. One dealing with ordinary trading revenues and expenditure including such items as materials, stationery, postages, rent and rates, sales, VAT and wages, is termed the *nominal ledger*. The second, the *private ledger* deals with those items which are acquired by the business but not intended for re-sale—land, buildings, plant, machines, desks, typewriters – and with loans, shares, dividends, etc.

Specimen ruling of an account All accounts in the several ledgers will have similar rulings and there are standard forms available. A commonly used type of ruling is illustrated in Figure 5.13. The principles followed in compiling the accounts are explained in later paragraphs.

It is probable that the accountant will recommend that the system of book-keeping known as the double-entry system should be used. For owners who intend to maintain effective control of the business it is prudent to accept this advice, and to start off with a well-

Figure 5.13 *Ruling of an account*

Account name					*A/C No SL* 19
Date		*fo*	*DR*	*CR*	*Balance*
1.1.1982	Balance b/d				125.00
4.1.1982	Invoice 157	SDBI	40.00		165.00
12.1.1982	Cheque	CB5		125.00	40.00

designed double-entry system, and not be tempted to take short cuts.

The fundamental principle of the double-entry system requires that every transaction is recorded twice. First it is looked at from the viewpoint of the account which has received the benefit of the transaction; for example when John Smith Ltd has received goods on credit from our business, the account of John Smith Ltd must show that value has been received to the extent of the sum of money stated on the invoice. The second way of regarding the transaction is from the viewpoint of the account giving the benefit. When John Smith Ltd was supplied with the goods the sales account gave value to the same amount (plus the VAT amount) as that received by the account of John Smith Ltd. In accountancy terms, the account receiving the benefit is debited with the amount, while the account giving the benefit is credited. To the layman this meaning of the words debit and credit may appear to be the opposite to their normal meaning in everyday speech. However, once the concept is grasped the double-entry system should be relatively simple to understand.

Let us follow through the various debit entries and credit entries in the transaction with John Smith Ltd.

An invoice is sent to John Smith Ltd for goods supplied to the value of £100 plus VAT of £15, an invoice total of £115.

The details of value of the invoice are entered into the sales daybook (See Figure 5.9). All the information necessary is thus contained in the sales daybook and from this the ledgers can be written up as follows:

Personal ledger - debtor section	– *Debit* the personal account of John Smith Ltd by £115
Impersonal ledger–nominal section	– *Credit* the Sales Account with £100 and *credit* the VAT account with £15.

The ledger now shows that the business has effected sales of £100, that John Smith Ltd owes the business £115 and the business owes £15 to the government for VAT.

John Smith Ltd in due course sends a cheque for £115 in settlement of the account. The value of the cheque is entered in the cash book as a debit (i.e. on the receipts side as shown in figure 5.10) and the account of John Smith Ltd is credited with £115.

The ledger now shows these entries:

	Dr	Cr
Sales account	–	100
Cash account	115	–
VAT account	–	15
John Smith Ltd account	115	115

In due course the business discharges the VAT liability with a payment by cheque for £15. The cheque is credited in the cash book (payments side) and the VAT account is debited with £15. The ledger now shows the entries as:

	Dr	Cr
Sales account	–	100
Cash account	115	15
VAT account	15	15
John Smith Ltd account	115	115

So the *balances* left in the various accounts at this stage are:

	Dr	Cr
Sales	–	100
Cash	100	–
VAT	–	–
John Smith Ltd	–	–

It will be noted that the cash book plays a dual role in the system of accounts. It has already been classified as a book of original entry. Now, in the example of the transaction with John Smith Ltd, it appears as an account in the double-entry system. The terms cash book and cash account can thus be regarded as synonymous.

This process will be repeated for every transaction the business undertakes whether dealing with sales, purchases, cheques received or cheques given in settlement. In consequence the ledgers will contain very many entries, and this means that there is a real possibility of errors occurring. To detect and correct any errors it is essential that the ledgers are balanced frequently. This means that all the debit and all the credit balances in the accounts have to be totalled. If these two totals are the same we have established that the value of all debit entries equals the value of all credit entries. If the totals are not the same a search of all the accounts must be made to find where the mistake occurred.

Even when they are the same, there is still the possibility that a transaction has been recorded on the wrong side of two accounts.

For example, in the earlier example the sales account could by mistake have been debited, and the account of John Smith Ltd credited. However this mistake would have been discovered when the cheque was received and further entries made. This periodical balancing is termed a *trial balance*.

The purpose of this chapter has been to indicate to the potential owner the process by which the books of account are kept. It is not the intention to make him into a competent book-keeper. However, in many very small firms, there will be no one else to keep the books. Too many people in these circumstances are content to leave the accountant to make up the books at various intervals, or at the time of the preparation of the annual audit. This means that the accountancy fee is greatly increased, and, even worse, that the owner has no indication during the year of how the business is progressing. The advice to anyone in this position must be to undergo a study course in book-keeping, perhaps at a local technical college, then to consult with their professional adviser about what books and ledgers should be kept. The aims should be to meet the needs of the owner in controlling the business and at the same time to satisfy statutory obligations.

Later on, as the number of transactions increases, it may be advisable to employ accounting machines in the book-keeping process. Provided the process is understood and the system is thoroughly established the owner can, when necessary, move to these aids even to using a microcomputer. But it is certainly inadvisable to go straight to the mechnical or electronic devices before mastering the basic procedures.

A pictorial representation of the book-keeping process is given in Figure 5.14.

Now that we have covered what may be called the mechanics of keeping the accounts we can move on to the use of these procedures in producing accounts to meet the statutory requirements and the needs of management. These topics form the subject of the following chapters.

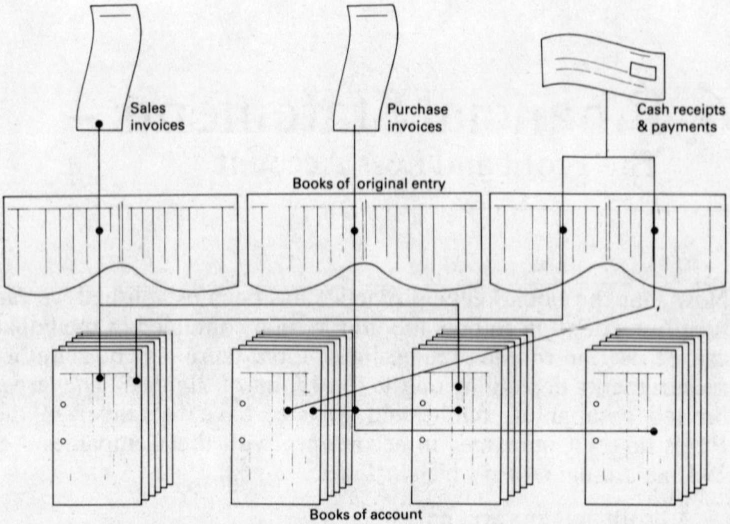

Figure 5.14 *The flow of accounting information*

6 Financial Statements – The Profit and Loss Account

Now that the book-keeping practice has been established we can turn our attention to how the information contained in the books can be used in running the business. First, there may be statutory requirements depending on the legal form of the firm. The larger limited companies, public and private, have to render to the Registrar of Companies in accordance with the Companies Act 1981 an annual return which includes:

A profit and loss account,
A balance sheet, and
A source and application statement.

The sole trader and the partnership are not affected by the Companies Act, while the only statement that small limited companies, as defined below, have to render is an abridged form of balance sheet. In order to be exempt from the requirement to submit a profit and loss account with the balance sheet a company must conform to two of the following three criteria:

Annual sales turnover not exceeding	£1,400,000
Total assets not exceeding	£700,000
Average number of employees during the year not exceeding	50

It will be obvious therefore that very few owners setting-up in business for the first time will be legally required to prepare any but the most limited amount of accounting information. However, this does not mean that the firm should not have proper accounts prepared. Two needs still remain: first, the Inland Revenue has to be satisfied that the profit reported, whether by sole trader, partnership or limited company, is true. Secondly, and perhaps more importantly, the owner(s) need accounting information prepared in such a manner that they can see how the business is faring.

If this information is lacking, unsound decisions may be made and wrong actions taken. The result may be that any profit made will be inadequate to meet the owners' objectives.

The Trading and Profit and Loss Account

Starting with the Inland Revenue, the information which will satisfy most of their needs is contained in the *trading and profit and loss account*. As its name suggests, this account presents a record of the results of trading during the year, and the profit or loss made in the course of trading. (The word 'year' in this context refers to the financial year, which can finish at any date chosen by the firm and thus does not necessarily coincide with the calendar year.)

A basic lay-out of this account is illustrated in Figure 6.1. It shows the revenue generated by sales and other activities of the company, and all the expenses incurred in operating the business during the financial year. All these figures, with the exception of the closing stocks of materials, have been recorded in the nominal ledger and shown in the trial balance (See p. 78). Two items in this example call for explanation: the method of calculating the value of materials used, and the word depreciation.

Materials used – this refers to materials used directly in producing the product or providing a service. For example, it would include such items as the timber used by the furniture maker, or the switches, cables, etc. used by the electrician. In order to establish the value of materials used it will be necessary to value the stock in hand at the close of the trading period. This value is ascertained by a physical stock check. So the closing stock figure for one year is the opening stock for the next year. The value of materials bought during the year is taken from materials account (or summation of several accounts for different materials) in the nominal ledger. A detailed explanation of the calculation outlined in the example is as follows:

Value of materials in stock at start of the year	10000
Add cost of purchases made during the year	54000
Thus value of materials available for use during the year is:	64000
Subtract value of stocks at the end of the year	8000
Then value of materials used during the year is:	56000

Figure 6.1 *Trading and profit and loss account for the year ending 31 March 1982*

			£
Sales Revenue			160 000
Direct costs			
Materials – Opening stock	10 000		
Purchases	54 000		
	64 000		
Less – Closing stock	8 000		
Materials used		56 000	
Wages		40 000	96 000
Gross Profit			64 000
Overhead expenses			
Salaries		28 000	
Rates		2 500	
Electricity		2 000	
Water		100	
Packing materials		800	
Carriage		1 600	
Loose tools		300	
Repairs – plant and equipment		1 800	
Postage and telephone		850	
Stationery		400	
Commission		2 000	
Advertising		1 250	
Travelling expenses		750	
Interest		1 200	
Insurance		1 200	
Professional charges		450	
Depreciation		3 800	
			49 000
Net profit before tax			15 000

Depreciation – In theory this figure represents the diminution over a period of time, in monetary terms, of the value of the buildings, machines, tools, motor-cars and other such items which are necessary in carrying on the business, but which are not used up in producing the goods or service (in accountancy terms the *fixed assets*). One formula (known as the diminishing balance) for assessing the amount of depreciation is stated in terms of percentages of the value of the different assets. For example the percentage allowed for buildings might be 2 per cent of their value, for machines 10 per cent and for motor-cars 15 per cent. (These are only examples and must not be read as a guide because the detail will differ from firm to firm.) Another method, preferred by management accountants, is the straight-line method which reduces the value of the asset each year by fixed instalments. The interest of the Inland Revenue in this figure lies in the fact that the profits declared will be different depending on which method is used. For example, the charge for depreciation of an asset late in its effective life will be greater under the straight-line method than under the diminishing balance method. This will be reflected in a lower declared profit, which has to be agreed by the Inland Revenue for the assessment of tax.

The businessman may find that the amounts allowed for depreciation are insufficient when looking at the cost of replacement of assets. It may, therefore, be prudent to provide for extra depreciation when establishing costs which he may wish to be reflected in selling prices.

The meaning of the other new terms in this example – direct costs, overhead expenses, and gross profit – will be obvious from the context in which they are used.

The lay-out shown in Figure 6.1 leaves much to be desired as a provider of information for managing the business. A far better lay-out is as shown in Figure 6.2. In this the overhead expenses have been grouped so that the owner can assess the relative costs of the various activities of the business. This could be the first step towards taking action to reduce any costs which appear to be too high.

The Operating Statement

Many owners are content to rely solely on the annual profit and loss account to keep them informed as to the progress of the business. This attitude can lead to unpleasant surprises when the final accounts are prepared, usually some months after the end of the financial year. What the person managing any business really needs is a report produced more frequently, perhaps with less accuracy than the annual accounts, but produced very soon after the period to be reported upon. Usually a monthly report is adequate and its preparation should not involve too much work; some businesses find that a three-monthly report is appropriate to their needs while others may find that it must be produced weekly.

This regular more frequent report is usually termed an *operating*

Figure 6.2 *Trading and profit and loss account for the year ending 31 March 1982*

			£
Sales			160 000
Direct costs			
Materials – Opening stock	10 000		
Purchases	54 000		
	64 000		
Less – Closing stock	8 000		
Usage		56 000	
Wages		40 000	96 000
Gross profit			64 000
Overhead expenses			
Production			
Salaries	12 000		
Repairs, Plant & equipment	1 800		
Water	100		
Electricity	2 000		
Depreciation	3 800		
Rates	2 500		
Loose tools	300	22 500	
Administration			
Salaries	16 000		
Postage & telephone	750		
Stationery	400		
Interest	1 200		
Insurance	1 200		
Professional charges	450	20 000	
Selling & distribution			
Commission	2 000		
Advertising	1 250		
Carriage	1 600		
Packing materials	800		
Travel expenses	850	6 500	
			49 000
Net profit before tax			15 000

statement so called to distinguish it from the year-end profit and loss account; the aim should be to have it produced within a few days of the end of the period to which it refers. Speed in preparation is more important than strict accuracy so it will probably be necessary to make estimates of some of the figures which are not readily available. For example, a manager of a manufacturing business might find that a physical check of stock every month is uneconomical, but would probably be able to assess the value of the stock in hand accurately enough to calculate the value of materials used.

The lay-out of the operating statement is similar to that of the trading and profit and loss account. The costs under some headings, for example commissions, packing materials, stationery, may be the actual sum invoiced during the period. Others such as rates, insurance, professional charges, might have to be estimated and apportioned over the months (or other periods) of the year. The figure for wages and salaries actually paid would be increased to allow for holiday pay being accrued but not yet paid. Thus, while it is not absolutely accurate, a statement can be prepared in good time to allow the owner to take any necessary corrective action should the sales level, incidence of costs, or profit, not be as anticipated.

Fixed and Variable Costs

There is another way of regarding costs which helps us to produce even more meaningful operating statements. If the example in Figure 6.2 is studied it will be apparent that many of the costs have been incurred directly in making the goods or providing the service. For example the materials were bought to be converted to the products which resulted in sales being made – the wages would have been paid to the machinists producing the articles for sale or to the carpenter fitting the doors in the house being built; the electricity might have been used entirely for providing power to drive the machines making the product. Such costs will tend to increase as activity increases – reflected in higher sales volumes – and tend to decrease with decreased activity. In short, they would be more or less in proportion to the volume of output. These costs are termed *variable costs*.

In the same example there are other costs which do not change for relatively small changes in the volume of output. (They might change for other reasons such as increased prices, but not as a result of increased activity.) Examples are rates, office salaries, professional charges and depreciation. These costs are termed *fixed costs*. Some costs, such as travelling expenses or water, might not fit neatly into either of these two categories; in practice it is usually possible to regard such costs either as more or less independent of volume and hence categorised as fixed or as more or less proportional to volume and hence categorised as variable.

The value of this categorisation into variable and fixed costs when compiling the operating statement will be seen in the example in Figure 6.3.

With this form of presentation of the figures the owner or manager is able every month to check quickly that the variable costs do in fact vary with the volume of sales. Any change from month to month in the proportion of variable costs to sales gives a warning signal that something might be wrong, leading to further investigation and corrective action. In addition to this the owner may regularly monitor the surplus left from the sales revenue after the variable costs are deducted. This surplus, known in the management accounting profession as the *contribution*, must obviously be large enough to meet all fixed costs and yield an adequate profit. An added benefit of this lay-out is that if the proprietor is satisfied that the fixed costs are reasonable stable the monthly statement could finish at the line showing the contribution. It might be adequate to report the fixed costs at three-or six-monthly intervals.

While the value of this approach has been shown by reference to the operating statement it will of course be equally useful to adopt the same form for the annual trading and profit and loss account prepared for management purposes.

The Profit Graph

The segregation of costs into variable and fixed costs allows further valuable information to be gained from the accounts. It makes it possible to determine the relationship between volume of sales and profit, that is, the effect on profit of an increase or decrease in sales revenue. This is most easily shown by constructing a profit graph, as demonstrated in Figure 6.4. This graph is sometimes referred to as the break-even chart for reasons which will be obvious when the method of interpreting the graph is understood.

The graph is drawn to show on the vertical axis the sales revenue and costs for the year and on the horizontal axis the sales volume or sales revenue. The graph in Figure 6.4 uses the figures given in the

Figure 6.3 *Operating statement for the month ending 30 November 1982*

Sales			14 000
Variable costs			
Materials	5 000		
Wages	3 500		
Electricity	150		
Commission	200		
Carriage	150		
Packing materials	100		
Repairs	150		
			9 250
Surplus			4 750
Fixed costs			
Production			
Salaries	1 000		
Water	100		
Rates	200		
Loose tools	50		
Depreciation	300		
		1 650	
Administration			
Salaries	1 300		
Postage & telephone	100		
Stationery	50		
Interest	100		
Insurance	100		
Professional charges	50		
		1 700	
Selling and distribution			
Advertising	100		
Travelling expenses	100		
		200	
Total fixed costs			3 550
Net profit before tax			1 200

Figure 6.4 *The profit graph*

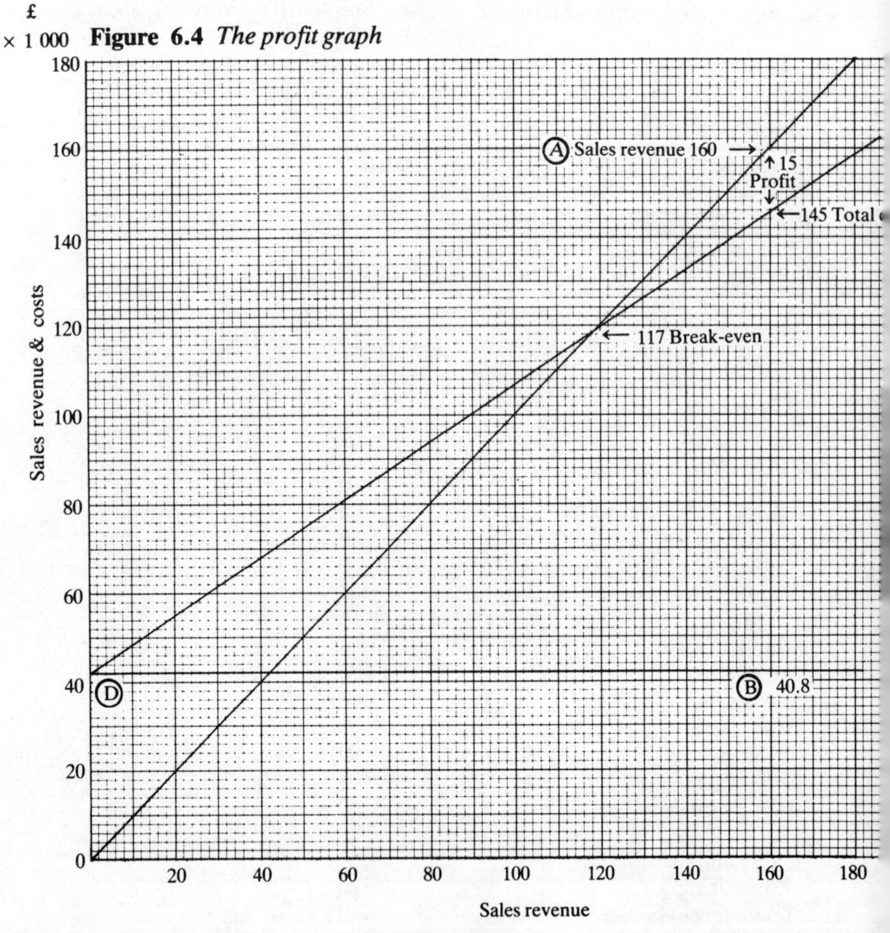

sample trading and profi and loss account (Figure 6.1). The costs are divided between the fixed and variable costs in the same way as demonstrated in the operating statement in Figure 6.2. The figures used in constructing the graph in in the illustration are:

Sales	160 000
Total variable costs	104 200
Total fixed costs	40 800
Profit	15 000

At £160,000 sales revenue on the horizontal axis there will clearly be a figure of £160,000 sales revenue to be plotted on the vertical axis (point A). This gives one point on the sales line. The line marked 'sales' can thus be drawn by joining the zero point to point A.

As previously stated it is reasonable to expect the fixed costs to remain fixed at any level of sales so a line may be drawn representing fixed costs at £40,800, from point B to point D.

At sales of £160,000 the variable costs are £104,200 and if this figure is added to the fixed costs we arrive at total costs of £145,000 at this volume of sales (point C on the graph). Now at zero sales there should be zero variable cost, in other words total costs and fixed costs are the same. A line can thus be drawn from point C to point D to show the total cost at any given level of sales.

A study of the resulting chart will show that up to a sales level of £117,000 costs are higher than revenue. This means that with the existing pattern of costs and sales the firm is making a loss up to this sales level. Above £117,000 sales the total costs are less than the sales revenue and so a profit is being generated. For this reason the point where the sales line crosses the total cost line is termed the break-even point. From this graph it is now possible to forecast the profit or loss which will accrue from any specified level of sales. There is one important proviso however. The pattern of sales, sometimes referred to as the sales mix, may change if new products are introduced, existing products are withdrawn, or there is a change in the relative levels of sales for different products.

Using this type of graph it is also possible to forecast the effect of changes in the cost structure, arising from changes in the expenses classified as fixed cost or those classified as variable costs. For example, Figure 6.5 shows that the effect of an increase in fixed costs of £10,000, with no increase in revenue and no change in variable cost, would be to move the break-even point to £145,000. It

Figure 6.5 *Fixed costs increased by £10 000*

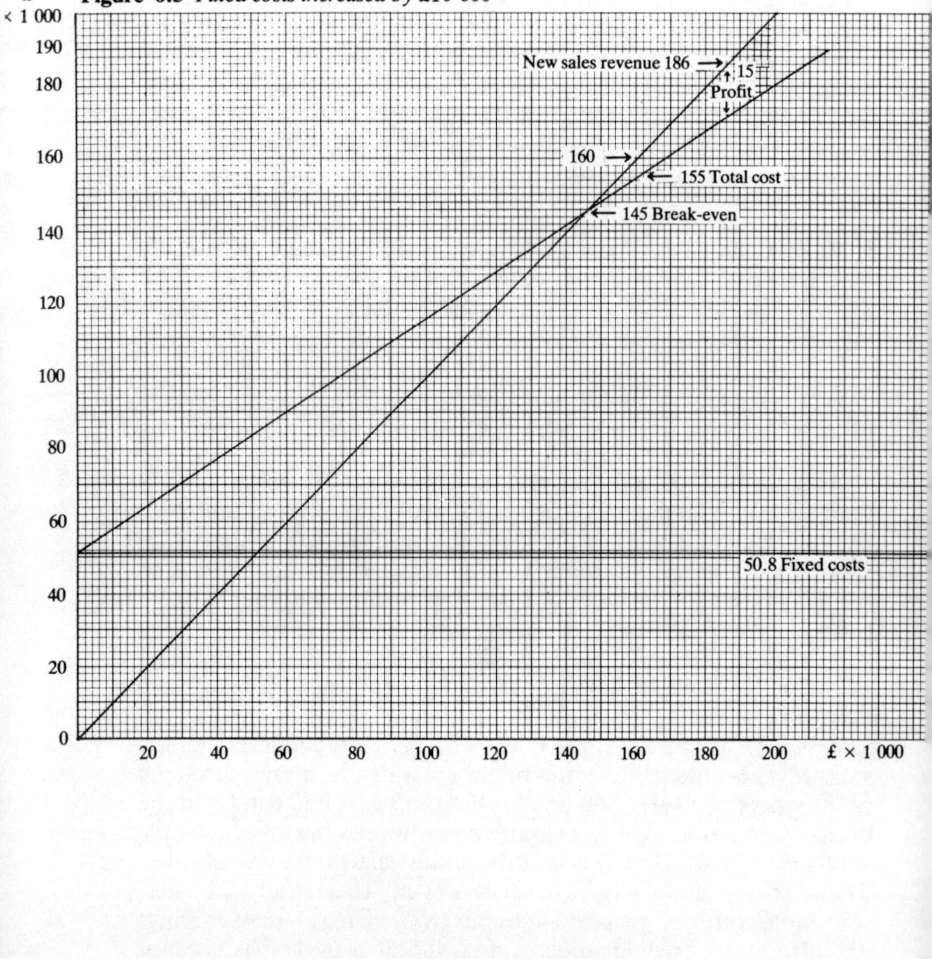

can also be read from the graph that in order to generate the same profit as before with unchanged prices a new level of sales of £186,000 must be achieved.

Looking at another possibility, that the variable costs increase by £10,000 while the fixed costs and sales revenue remain unchanged at their previous levels, we see from Figure 6.6 that the break-even point has moved to £143,000. If the original profit is to be achieved sales would have to increase to £196,000. From this it can be seen that while it might be possible, it may be difficult to compensate for cost increases by increasing sales volume. Further, if the rise in costs occurs because of increased variable costs the task is made even more difficult.

In some circumstances it may be possible to restore the original profit only by raising prices or by a combination of increased volume and increased prices.

We now have the means at our disposal to develop plans for a given level of profit. Before the profit graph was constructed, the trading and profit and loss account and the operating statements already provided information which was invaluable. However, it did not allow us to predict the possible consequences of changing the cost structure of the business, or of changing the pattern of sales. The profit graph meets this need.

However, before pursuing this topic further it is necessary to look into the question of what level of profit the business should be aiming for. In order to assess this level it is desirable to consider first the other two financial statements – the *balance sheet* and the *source and application statement* – which are the subjects of Chapter 7.

Figure 6.6 *Variable costs increased by £10 000*

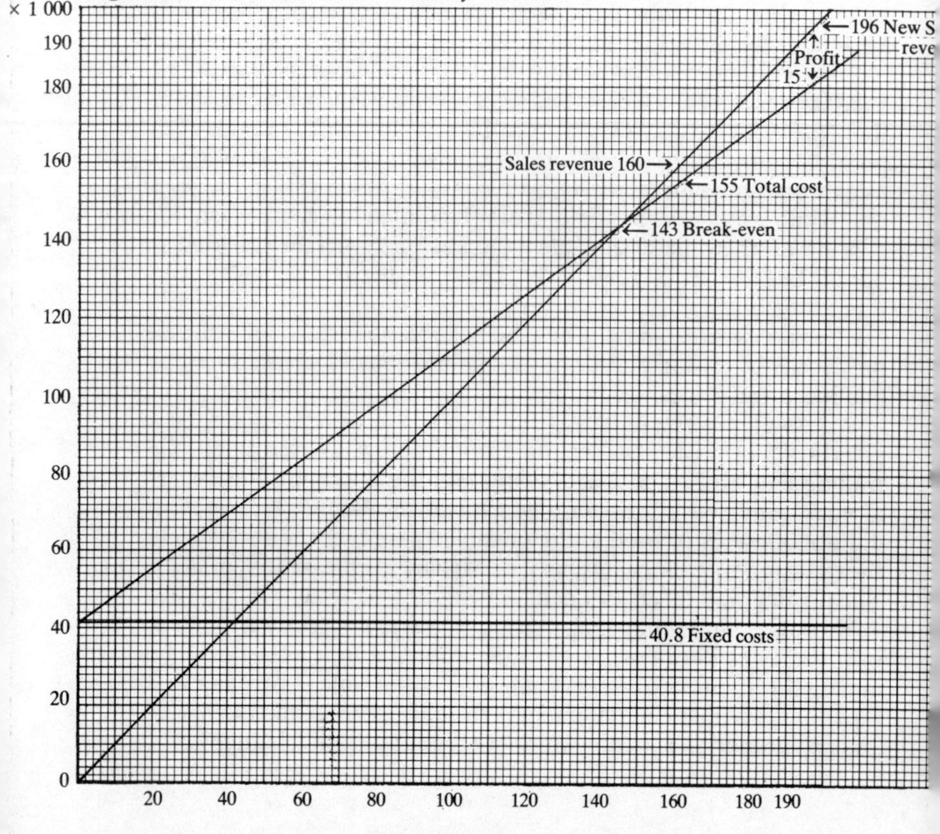

7 Financial Statements – The Balance Sheet and the Source and Application Statement

It may appear at first sigh that the balance sheet has little relevance to most firms at the start-up stage except, as indicated earlier, to present a forecast for the bank manager or other lender. However, the subject does warrant a study. The private limited company has a legal obligation to submit a balance sheet as at the end of each year's trading. More importantly, the information it contains offers some guidance when deciding longer-term policies.

The purpose of the balance sheet is to present a picture of the funds employed in a business – where they came from, and how they are being used. This picture is taken at a definite time on a definite date. It may for example be at the close of trading on 31 December, 31 January, 31 March, or whatever year-end date has been chosen by the firm.

Form of Presentation

Many people find it difficult to understand the balance sheet in the form in which it is presented by most companies nowadays. It may be helpful, therefore, in explaining the subject, to refer first to the earlier form which has now been superseded by the modern style of presentation. The earlier form presents the information as illustrated in Figure 7.1. This shows a simple statement prepared for a limited company for management purposes, and the company chosen for this example is the one for which the trading and profit and loss account was prepared (Figure 5.13). Partnerships and sole traders would use a slightly different layout, but the principles are the same.

Figure 7.1 *Balance sheet – old form*

Balance sheet at 31 March 1982

Liabilities	£	£	*Assets*	£	£
Capital			Fixed assets		
Share capital	12 000		Land & buildings	50 000	
Revenue reserves	58 000	70 000	Plant & equipment	15 000	
			Fixtures & fittings	1 000	
Loan capital		5 000	Vehicle	4 000	
		75 000			70 000
Current liabilities			Current assets		
Creditors &			Stock	5 000	
provisions	14 000		Work-in-progress	2 000	
Bank overdraft	5 500		Finished goods	1 000	
Tax provisions	9 000		Debtors	26 000	
Proposed dividend	1 000		Cash in hand	500	
		29 500			34 500
		104 500			104 500

The terms liabilities and assets may be confusing to the layman so it may be advisable for the moment to consider the two sides as detailing what funds are used in the business and where they came from. If right-hand side is examined, it will be seen that all the items listed show how the funds invested in the business have been used.

Starting with the fixed assets there are details of buildings, plant, etc. which have a total value of £70,000. This value, termed the *net book value*, represents the purchase price of the asset, less the depreciation which has been charged in the profit and loss account for each year since the asset was acquired.

The next heading – current assets shows how much of the funds are tied up in the working capital:

Stocks of raw materials are valued at £5000
Work going through the process but not yet finished is valued at £2000
Finished goods are held in stock to a total value of £1000

The firm has sent out invoices to its customers, but has not yet received payment – the firm is in effect lending its customers £26,000. Cash in hand amounts to £500.

The term current assets is applied to these items to distinguish them from the fixed assets of the business. It will be seen that they are either consumed in, or are used to finance, the day-to-day activities of the business.

The left-hand side shows where the funds came from to finance the fixed and current assets.

Capital – The share capital is the sum which the owners have invested in the business in the shares of the company for £12,000.

The item 'revenue reserves' needs a little more explanation. This business has in the past earned profits, of which £58,000 has not been paid out in dividends, but kept in the firm and used in the financing of new fixed assets and working capital. These retained profits are termed the *revenue reserves*. This is a rather misleading term because it tends to suggest that cash has been put away for use later on. In fact it will be seen that the only cash in this particular company at this date is £500.

Loan capital, as its name suggests, shows that the company has borrowed, probably by long-term loans, a sum of £5000. The company will probably have had to provide security for this amount and also may have to pay interest on it.

Under the next heading, *current liabilities*, are listed the current short-term debts of the company. The firm has received materials or services to the value of £14,000 but has not yet paid for them. (The word 'provisions' is used to denote that goods or services have been received but that the invoices have not yet been received.)

In effect this means that the creditors are lending the firm money in the same way that the firm is lending money to its debtors. The bank has allowed the company to overdraw its account by £5500. There is a tax liability of £9000 which has not yet been paid. Finally, the company proposes to distribute to its shareholders a total of £1000 by way of a dividend.

The total of the side headed liabilities balances the total of the side headed assets, and of course, this must be so. All the assets on the right-hand side have come into being through the use of funds at one time or another. These funds must have come from one source or another and these sources are shown on the left-hand side. The heading liabilities is used because the business owes those sums to someone, either the shareholders or banks, other lenders, suppliers, or the Inland Revenue.

The style of presentation more commonly used in businesses today sets out the same information in a vertical form as shown in Figure 7.2. It will be noted that two new terms have been introduced.

Figure 7.2 *Balance sheet – current style*

Balance sheet as at 31 March 1982

	£	£	£
Fixed assets			
Land & builidngs		50 000	
Plant & equipment		15 000	
Fixtures & fittings		1 000	
Vehicles		4 000	
			70 000
Current assets			
Stocks of raw material	5 000		
Work-in-progress	2 000		
Finished goods	1 000		
Debtors	26 000		
Cash-in-hand	500		
		34 500	
Less current liabilities			
Creditors	14 000		
Bank overdraft	5 500		
Taxation	9 000		
Proposed dividend	1 000		
		29 500	
Net current assets			5 000
Net capital employed			75 000
Financed by			
Share capital	12 000		
Revenue reserves	58 000		
		70 000	
Loan		5 000	
			75 000

The surplus remaining when the current liabilities have been deducted from the current assets is termed *net current assets*. The total of fixed assets and net current assets is the *net capital employed*, a term which is used to indicate the amount of capital tied-up in the business in the long term.

Partnership accounts, while following the same principles, are usually laid out in the form illustrated in Figure 7.3. The differences between this form and that used for the limited liability company arises from the different legal status of the owners. The partnership,

Figure 7.3 *Balance sheet – partnership*

Balance sheet as at 31 March 1982

	£	£	£
Fixed assets			
Land & buildings		50 000	
Plant & equipment		15 000	
Fixtures & fittings		1 000	
Vehicles		4 000	70 000
Current assets			
Stocks of raw material	5 000		
Work-in-progress	2 000		
Finished goods	1 000		
Debtors	26 000		
Cash-in-hand and at bank	500	34 500	
Less current liabilities			
Creditors	14 000		
Bank overdraft	5 500		
Partnrs current A/cs			
X 6 000			
Y 2 000			
Z 2 000	10 000	29 500	
Net current assets			5 000
Capital employed			75 000
Financed by			
Partners capital accounts	X 30 000		
	Y 25 000		
	Z 20 000		75 000

of course, does not have shareholders and thus there will be no share capital nor dividends. Also, any tax liability is the individual responsibility of each of the partners, because the profit earned by the firm will have been shared on an agreed basis between the partners. Two new terms call for explanation. The *partners capital accounts* were established when the partners contributed sums of money to the business in accordance with the agreement referred to in chapter 4. Once the contributions by the individual partners have been established it is prudent to leave them undisturbed because they may be used as the basis for sharing profit. The *partners current accounts* are required so that shares of profits and any sums of money injected by the partners on a short-term basis can be recorded. Also recorded in this account are the drawings from the partnership by way of salary or withdrawal of all or part of the profits in accordance with the partnership agreement. The sums shown in Figure 7.3 represent the current balance in each partner's account.

A similar lay-out to that shown in Figure 7.3 would be used by a sole trader with the possible exception that, because all the funds belong to the same person, the amount on current account would be included in the capital account.

In chapter 6 the legal definition of a small limited liability company was given (p. 80). Companies which conform to that definition need only submit an abridged form of balance sheet. The layout is as shown in Figure 7.4, but it is not usual for any one company to need all the headings shown here. Each company will use those which are appropriate.

Some of the terms require explanation as they have not been referred to in the earlier descriptions. Under fixed assets there is *intangible assets*. This term is used when a company has had to make a permanent investment to start or develop the business, but for which nothing can be shown in tangible form. For example, the business may have been bought by its present owner from the previous owner for a sum of money which is greater than the balance sheet valuation. However, it may be worth the extra sum because a good reputation has been developed and the business has a number of well-established customers. This extra sum is termed *goodwill* and recorded in the balance sheet as an intangible asset.

Another example is provided by the business which incurred expenses prior to incorporation in the formation of the company. These expenses would include, among others, legal and professional expenses. These would be shown in the balance sheet as preliminary expenses.

The term *tangible assets* refers to the land, buildings, machines, etc. The words *prepayments* and *accrued income* refer to payments made in advance for which benefit has not yet been received, or income earned (for example, from investments) but not yet received.

It will be noted that the word *creditors* occurs twice. The first time it refers to payments falling due within one year of the date of the balance sheet, and this figure takes the place of the current liabilities shown in Figure 7.2.

Figure 7.4 *Balance sheet – Small limited liability company*

Balance sheet as at 31 March 1982

A. *Called up share capital not paid*
B. *Fixed assets*
   I intangible assets
   II tangible assets
   III investment

C. *Current assets*
   I stocks
   II debtors
   III investments
   IV cash

D. *Prepayments & accrued income*

E. *Creditors (due within 1 year)*

F. *Net current assets*

G. *Total assets less current liabilities*

H. *Creditors (due after 1 year)*
I. *Provision for liabilities & charges*
J. *Accruals & deferred income*

K. *Capital*
   I Called up share capital
   II Share premium account
   III Revaluation reserves
   IV Other reserves
   V Profit & loss account

(Note, The capital letters A, B, C etc and the Roman numerals I, II, III etc, are essential features of this presentation.)

The net current assets on this interpretation are:

	Current assets (C)
plus	Prepayments and accrued income (D)
minus	Creditors (due within one year) (E)

The second time the word appears it refers to payments which will not fall due within one year of the date of the balance sheet.

Provision for liabilities and charges covers such matters as obligations for pensions and taxes. *Accruals and deferred income* refers to items for which value has been received but for which payment is not yet due.

Capital. Under this heading there are two items, neither of which is likely to concern the company in its very early days:

Share premium account– When the company has been trading for some time the directors may decide to recommend an issue of more shares and to offer them at a higher price than the nominal value. To make this clearer let us assume that Company A has registered its share capital as £1000 in £1 shares, but has only issued 500 of the shares. If the business has prospered it could be that after a few years the profits earned will have increased the value of the business to the extent that certain people are prepared to pay, say, £2 for each share. But the nominal value of the extra shares as shown in the balance sheet will still be £1; the extra £1 received per share is accounted for by recording it in the share premium account.

Revaluation reserves – This term is used when the fixed assets of the company have been professionally revalued at a figure higher than that recorded in the books of account. As this means that the value of fixed assets on one side of the balance sheet as presented in Figure 7.1 has been raised, it is necessary to make a corresponding entry on the other side under the heading revaluation reserves (sometimes referred to as *capital reserve*).

Comparison between Figures 7.4 and 7.2 may suggest that this abridged form of balance sheet is more complicated than the conventional form. This is not so; Figure 7.2 was deliberately kept simple in order to explain the principles, whereas Figure 7.4 is the full form as laid down in the Companies Act 1981. However the directors may decide that the balance sheet prepared for management purposes is more appropriate to their needs and that the abridged form will be prepared only for submission to the Registrar of Companies.

Using the Information

Earlier, we said that some of the detailed figures in the balance sheet may prove of value to the manager when matters of policy are being considered. In fact, when read in conjunction with the trading and profit and loss account a great deal of information can be extracted by the calculation of certain relationships, and some pertinent questions may be answered. Some of these are discussed below.

Is the profit adequate?

The adequacy of profit may be assessed by measuring the pre-tax profit against the net capital employed. The term used for this relationship is *return on capital employed*, usually expressed as a percentage. In Figure 6.1 the profit was shown as £15,000 and in Figure 7.2 the capital employed was £75,000 so the return on capital was 20 per cent ($\frac{15{,}000}{75{,}000} \times 100$). The businessman may compare this 20 per cent with the rate which the same amount of money would earn if invested in some other way – with a building society, bank, local authority, or elsewhere in the money market. (This 20 per cent is equivalent to a net rate of 12 per cent at a small business tax rate of 40 per cent.) If the rate compares unfavourably, it may indicate that some past policies were not well conceived, and that some new thinking is called for. Some guidance may be offered by answering two further questions: Is the relationship of profit to sales adequate? Is too much capital being employed in the business?

Profit to sales

The adequacy of profit when related to sales is measured by comparing the net pre-tax profit with the sales achieved. As the sales revenue is £160,000 the return on sales is 9.4 per cent ($\frac{15{,}000}{160{,}000} \times 100$). However, this figure is only of value when it can be compared with past results, or with the results achieved by other businesses in a similar industry or trade. The new firm which has no past history might be able to get some idea of what may be expected by studying the published accounts of other companies in the same line of business. The larger library will probably have some information available in the form of record cards produced by some of the credit-monitoring agencies.

Is too much capital employed?

To answer this the relationship of sales to capital employed is calculated. In the examples given the sales were £160,000 and the capital £75,000. So the relationship is 2.1:1. It may be generally assumed that the higher the capital turnover the more likely it is that the company is successful. This is not necessarily so, because even a high capital turnover can, if coupled with a low return on sales, result in a low return on capital. The connection between these three relationships may be illustrated by a diagram:

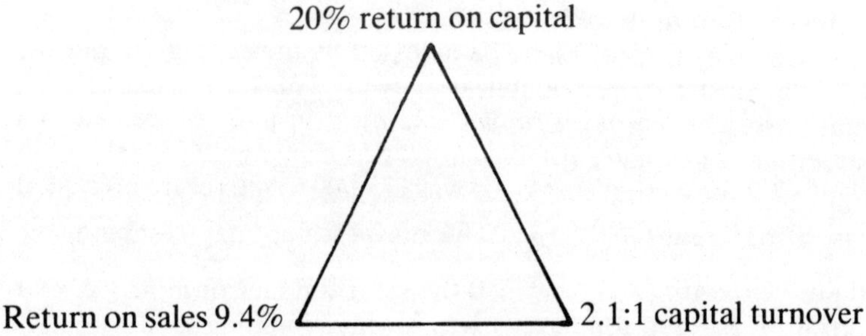

It will be seen that if the return on sales (9.4%) is multiplied by the capital turnover (2.1) the result is the return on capital. Again, this figure for capital turnover may be of little value unless it can be compared with past records, or with the results achieved in similar businesses.

When these three relationships have been calculated it may be decided that action is called for to improve the return on capital. This may be achieved in one or more of the following ways: (i) reduce the capital employed while maintaining the existing sales and profit performance; (ii) increase the volume of sales at the existing return on sales without increasing the capital employed; (iii) increase the prices so that the return on sales will be increased while the capital employed remained unchanged; (iv) reduce the costs while leaving sales and capital employed at the existing levels.

These relationships deal with the profitability of the business. Other information contained in the accounts may offer clues as to the soundness of the policies relating to the use of funds. In using this information a further series of relationships is established, usually referred to as *management ratios*.

Is the business solvent?

The business is said to be solvent if it can meet its current liabilities from its short-term assets. The position may be assessed from the balance sheet by calculating the *solvency ratio*. In Figure 7.2 the current assets are shown as £34,500 and the current liabilities as £29,500. The ratio is thus 34,500:29,500 (1.2:1).

This indicates that the current assets only just exceed the current liabilities. For safety, a ratio of at least 2:1 should be aimed for, because several of the current assets could not readily be converted to cash if all the trade creditors and the bank, etc. demanded settlement at short notice. A rider must be added to this statement however – in the partnership a large part of the liabilities may consist of the partners current accounts in which case the 2:1 requirement might not apply.

To check on the ability of the firm to pay its short-term debts a further ratio is usually calculated. Known as the *liquidity ratio* this is calculated as for the solvency ratio, except that the only assets (apart from cash) considered to be readily convertible to cash are those under the heading debtors. In the example, there is £26,000 + £500 available to meet the current liabilities. The ratio is thus 0.9 $\left(\frac{26{,}500}{29{,}500}\right)$ For safety this ratio should never be allowed to fall below 1.0 for long periods of time.

How long are customers taking to pay?

A useful measure of the effectiveness of credit control practice is provided by finding out how many weeks customers are taking, on average, to pay their accounts. This can be calculated quite simply. In the example, annual sales (52 weeks) amount to £160,000. The amount owed by debtors is £26,000. It follows therefore that, on average, the number of weeks represented by outstanding debts is 8½ $\left(\frac{26{,}000}{160{,}000} \times 52\right)$. If this figure is higher than the target set in making the cash flow forecast, some tightening of procedures may be called for, especially if the debtors are being financed by the overdraft.

Are stock levels of raw materials too high?

This question can be answered by calculating the length of time these stocks would last at existing rates of use. As the value of raw materials in stock is £5000 and the value of the quantity used in the past 52 weeks is £56,000, the answer is 4½ weeks $\left(\frac{5{,}000}{56{,}000} \times 52\right)$. A figure at this level would be considered by most businesses to be very satisfactory, provided that the delivery times offered by suppliers of materials are short enough to allow timely replenishment of stocks. A similar ratio may be calculated to monitor the level of finished stocks against the value of annual sales.

In addition to these ratios, the value of which lies in the guidance provided in operating the firm, there is one further ratio which needs to be monitored. This is the ratio of capital on which interest has to be paid (loans and overdrafts) to the capital on which interest does not have to be paid (provided by the shareholders or partners) usually referred to as the *gearing ratio*. In Figure 7.2 the capital on which interest is payable amounts to:

Loan	5 000
Overdraft	5 500
	10 500
The shareholder's funds are:	
Share capital	12 000
Revenue reserves	58 000
	70 000

This ratio (1:7) appears to be quite safe and in this example the company could quite safely increase its borrowings. The importance in achieving the right gearing lies in the fact that while there may be no difficulty in paying the interest on high borrowings when business is good, when business is bad the interest charges may be too great a burden. There are no hard and fast rules as to what this ratio should be, but it is generally accepted that interest-bearing capital should not be higher than the shareholders' funds.

To complete the review of the documents which should be prepared for management purposes one further statement must be included:

The Source and Application Statement

This statement provides a summary of the various ways in which funds have been used in the business during the year, and the sources from which the funds were obtained. The main purpose for which it is prepared is to explain to the management and shareholders how the profit earned during the year has been used, by illustrating the movement in funds which have taken place during the year.

Considering the company whose financial statements were illustrated in Figures 6.2 and 7.2 a very simple method of laying out the statement is as in Figure 7.5. It will be noted that net inflow of cash is £18,800 and not £15,000. This is because the £3800 charged for depreciation did not represent cash actually spent. (The other sums in Figure 7.5 would, in practice, be derived from a comparison of the balance sheet in Figure 7.2 with the balance sheet that would

Figure 7.5 *Source and application statement*

Source and application statement for year ending 31 March 1982

	£
Sources	
Internal	
Net inflow of cash	18 800
Decrease in stocks	2 000
External loans	–
Total inflow – all sources	20 800
Application	
New plant & equipment	1 000
Taxation paid	3 100
Dividends paid	1 200
Loans repaid	2 500
Increase in debtors	10 500
Decrease in creditors	1 500
Decrease in bank overdraft	800
	20 600
Net change = cash in hand	200

have been prepared at the end of the previous year. From these two balance sheets the changes in the value of assets and liabilities could be calculated.)

In practice the statement is usually laid out as on Figure 7.6. This shows the profit which was earned after depreciation had been allowed for, so depreciation has to be added back to arrive at the net inflow of cash. There is also a major change in the lay-out of the section headed applications. The items comprising working capital have been segregated from other items, and the decrease in stocks has been shown as a reduction in working capital rather than as a source of funds. The resulting statement shows clearly the change in working capital which has taken place during the year.

This statement is probably of greater use to companies engaged in manufacturing than to service businesses or retailers. However, as with all the topics described in this and earlier chapters each business must decide which management documents are relevant to its needs, in addition to the minimum demanded by the various authorities.

Figure 7.6 *Source and application statement for year ending 31 March 1982*

	£	£
Sources		
Internal – Pretax profit		15 000
Depreciation		3 800
External – Loans		–
Total all sources		18 800
Applications		
New plant & equipment	1 000	
Taxation	3 100	
Dividends	1 200	
Loan repayment	2 500	
		7 800
Changes in working capital		
Increase in debtors	10 500	
Decrease in creditors	1 500	
Decrease in bank overdraft	800	
	12 800	
Less decrease in stock	2 000	
Net increase in working capital		10 800
Total applications		18 600
Net change – cash in hand		200

8 Controlling the Cash

So far the steps necessary to set up and control the business have been dealt with, with the purpose of reaching a profit target. It is equally important to control the flow of cash into and out of the business. This means that an objective must be set. This might be, for example, that the overdraft and other borrowings will not exceed a certain figure in order that interest charges are kept to affordable levels. When the objective is clear the flows of cash must then be carefully monitored so that appropriate action may be taken at the right time to ensure that the objective is achieved. In this, perhaps even more than in the other activities, strict discipline is essential.

It is not difficult to set up a system to impose this necessary discipline when the firm has developed to the status of the private limited company with several employees. The company is legally a separate entity, and must keep proper accounts so that a base exists from which control procedures can be developed. The sole trader, on the other hand, is not subject to such rigid constraints because in law the person and the business are the same entity. Due to this lack of a legal distinction many sole traders allow their personal affairs to be merged into the affairs of the business, and fail to exercise necessary discipline.

The first step should be to separate business and personal accounts. Consider a family living in a holiday or tourist area, (and this example is not uncommon) where the husband runs a service business from home, perhaps carrying out roof repairs. The wife meanwhile is taking in paying guests, using the house as a guest house. In effect there are two separate businesses operating from premises in which the owners are also living with their family. For tax purposes the husband is probably regarded by the Inland Revenue as the recipient of all income from the two ventures and responsible for all expenditure incurred. If the husband and wife take the same view as the Inland Revenue, then all income will be pooled into a common fund from which all expenditure will be made whether or not it is incurred on behalf of the roofing business, the guest house or the normal day-to-day living expenses of the family. This family may not know whether the roofing business is subsidised by the guest house, or vice versa, or whether each business is generating enough income to support its separate existence. Incidentally, as well as perhaps causing occasional financial difficulties, this attitude could well lead to an unprofitable division of the owners' time between the two businesses and their private life.

The least that people in this position should do is to keep separate accounts. Revenues and expenditure for each would then be recorded separately, so that at frequent periods (weekly or monthly) the cash position of each could be monitored. Each account would also record payments paid to the owners (in accountancy terms, their *drawings*) and these sums would be regarded as payments out of the business, thereby reducing the net inflow of cash, or increasing the net outflow. It might even be advisable to open separate bank accounts for the businesses and a personal one for the family. If this is done, of course, the owners should be careful that they do not incur interest charges by allowing any of the accounts to be overdrawn. A further measure of discipline which must be self-imposed is to resist the temptation to allow cash payments from customers to be spent for any reason without the fact being properly recorded. It is a sensible precaution to pay all income into the bank account and to draw out regularly a wage for the owners, any payments on behalf of the businesses being made by cheque.

Continuing with the same example, the roof repairer may, on occasion, take on jobs which will take a long time – perhaps weeks – to complete, but for which he has had to buy materials, and perhaps engage a temporary employee. These are added reasons for keeping a separate account for the business. He now has a customer who owes his business money (a debtor), and if he is well-established as a reliable trader, he might have bought his materials on credit terms, so that he also has creditors. Without a proper system of accounting his affairs could easily become very confused. He also has to pay his employee promptly which might cause his accounts to show a net outflow of cash; the knowledge of this might stimulate him to negotiate progress payments with his customers.

The shopkeeper offers another example of the need to exercise strict control of cash. The temptation here is to take money from the till for personal expenditure without making proper records. The owner who gets into this habit runs the risk of not having the cash to pay his bills for goods when they come in from his suppliers. As with the roof repairer/guest house businessses it is much wiser to pay all cash takings into the bank and draw out a regular salary, or at the very least keep proper records in which any drawings are entered scrupulously.

There is another trap into which the unwary retailer may fall – granting credit. The small shopkeeper must have a strict policy on this matter, and keep to it. In general, the rule should be that all goods are sold for cash and no credit given. The extreme example of good cash management is provided by the supermarkets. All goods are sold for cash, probably even before the supermarket has paid its suppliers for the goods. The small corner shopkeeper may not reach this ideal state; the goods may still remain on the shelves after the suppliers have been paid. But at least he can avoid making matters worse by allowing credit. There are some shops, of course, where credit has to be allowed, for example, the newsagent who offers a delivery service. The rule must be to set a fixed limit to the time allowed for payment, preferably a weekly settlement or at most monthly, and then to refuse further credit. There can be no excuse for allowing credit to be extended to six months or more, yet many shopkeepers allow this to happen because of fear of losing custom.

When the position of the manufacturer or other larger-scale enterprise, which has to rely on taking and giving credit, is considered the need for adequate cash control systems is much clearer. In this sort of venture the legitimate pursuit of profit can lead to a shortage of cash unless the business is kept under firm control. The distinction between cash and profit is not always clearly appreciated. This was one of the reasons for failure of the unsuccessful venturer described in chapter 1. He was funding the purchase of materials and paying wages by injecting first his own cash into the firm, and then by arranging an overdraft. Each of his contracts with his customer proved to be profitable, but the rapid expansion of the business required more cash than was being generated from profit. At the same time, he was allowing a longer period of credit to his customer than he was allowed by his suppliers. When the customer ran into financial difficulties his cash resources were inadequate to tide his business over. Had this man made a cash flow forecast on the lines suggested in chapter 3 the danger of his position would have been seen much earlier. He might have insisted on very much stricter terms of payment with his customer; he might even have not accepted the orders for larger quantities. Many businessmen find it very difficult to refuse an order, and yet it is sometimes essential to do so for the survival of the company. Perhaps one rule to follow is not to risk more than the company can afford to lose without becoming insolvent. Another general rule illustrated by this example is not to have too many eggs in one basket. If the owner had limited his trade with any one customer to, say, a quarter or a third of his total business, he might have maintained a cash flow adequate to see the company through the crisis.

Working Capital

A convenient term for defining the cash and other funds used in the day-to-day operations of the business is *working capital*. To illustrate the concept, the diagram in Figure 8.1 shows the working capital employed in a manufacturing business as a cycle. It starts with an inflow of funds to finance operations, followed by various outflows until, if all goes well, a surplus is left which returns to continue the cycle. Clearly, if the cash flow in the business is to be controlled two requirements have to be met. First, the time elapsing between the start and finish of the cycle must be limited, and secondly the volume of outflow must be controlled. To see what measures may be taken to achieve these ends it will be helpful to analyse the cycle into its components.

Creditors

Obviously it will improve a company's cash balance if payment to creditors is delayed for as long as is reasonably possible. Large firms can sometimes negotiate, or even take without negotiation, extended credit because the value of their orders is high enough to make them valuable customers. This course is rarely open to the small firm because its orders are usually of relatively low value. In general, it is prudent for the small firm to take the credit which has been agreed and to pay at the end of that period. The goodwill of suppliers can be extremely important; a consistently poor paying record could result in a reluctance on the part of the supplier to supply goods on credit. On the other hand, it is not unknown for suppliers to agree to several months' credit to help a customer whose record of payment has been consistently good. The questions of discounts for prompt payment also needs careful thought. A discount of 2½ per cent for settlement within, say, two weeks instead of a normal period of perhaps six weeks really means that the supplier is offering interest to the customer at an annual rate of about 30 per cent. The value of

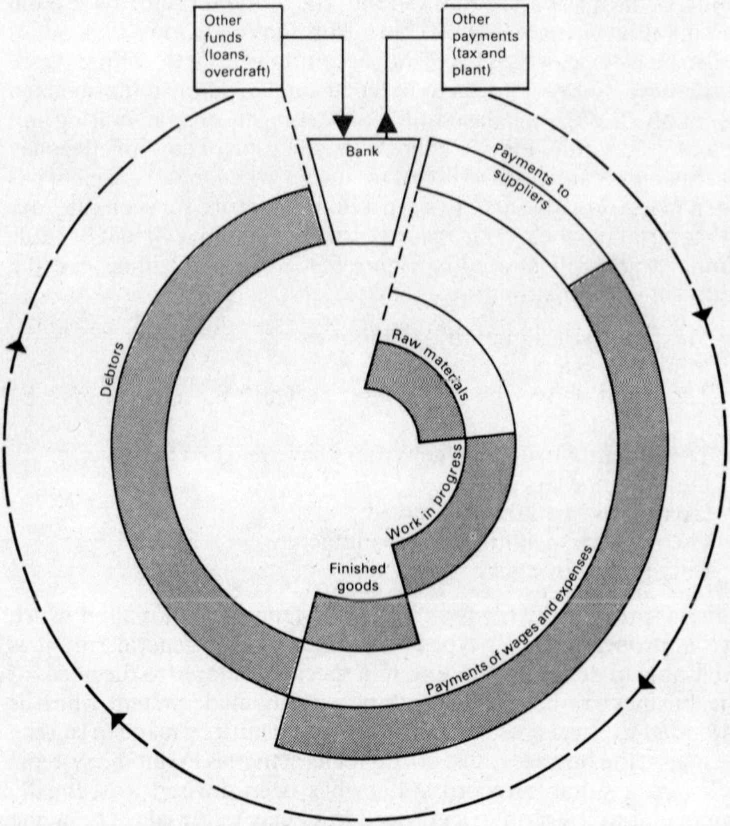

Figure 8.1 *The working capital cycle*

this would, of course, have to be balanced against the loss of the cash in the business for four weeks.

If the owner is to ensure that maximum value is to be obtained from the credit allowed without alienating suppliers it is well worth setting up a simple reminder system. The rule should be to pay on time, but not earlier than is necessary. This rule, of course, applies not only to payments to suppliers of materials but to suppliers of services and to local authorities.

Raw Materials

For this part of the cycle the aim must be to control volume and value both of raw materials held in stock, and those being used in the manufacturing process. This means that there must be a policy regarding stocks which takes into account three factors. First, there is the need to keep stocks to meet customers' likely requirements. Secondly, there is the desirability of keeping the manufacturing unit running smoothly. Finally, there is the question of how much money the business can afford to invest in stocks. When this assessment has been made it is advisable to keep a running record for each category of material in stock. This record, usually kept on a system of cards similar to that illustrated in Figure 5.3, would contain at least the following information:

Maximum stock quantity permitted.
Minimum safety level of stocks.
The point above the safety level at which more stock must be ordered.
The quantity to order when stocks have reached this level.
Details of orders placed.
Quantities of material received.
Quantities issued for use in manufacture.
Balance left in stock.

Several proprietary cards and other systems exist, not all of which are appropriate to all types of business. As a general rule it is advisable to devise a simple system specially tailored to the needs of the business rather than to adopt a ready-made system which is intended to cover a wider field. The system must be made to suit the business; the business must not adapt its activities to suit the system.

When a suitable record system has been devised it is equally important to insist on strict procedures being followed covering the ordering, receipt, inspection, issue and use of materials. In many types of business the cost of raw materials is a very large part of total cost, and carelessness in dealing with them can lead to higher costs of operation and increased outflows of cash.

The other requirement is that materials must move quickly round the cycle. They should not be worked on any sooner than will be necessary to meet customers' requirements. When started, the work should move quickly through the cycle so that the materials are converted into finished goods and sold. This means that production must be planned and controlled. This matter is dealt with in chapter 11.

Labour

The manufacturing company will almost certainly be employing people to make the product and administer the commercial activities. This is one of the major costs in most companies so it is a resource which must be used effectively. The people must be selected wisely, trained to do the work effectively and to specified standards of quality, and be encouraged to put in a good effort. Equally important, their work must be properly organised so that they can be kept fully occupied. This again relies on the productive process being planned and controlled, and materials being available at the right time. More will be said about managing people in chapter 12.

Finished Goods

Some companies find it necessary to maintain a stock of finished goods to meet the customers demands promptly. A typical example of this would be the manufacturer of small engineering fitments which are used by other manufacturers in repairing their machines. These customers may want delivery at very short notice, so the company with stock in hand will get the order. Another example, on a smaller scale, would be the small pottery which has to maintain stocks to meet the demands of retail customers or visiting tourists. The same principles apply as for maintaining stocks of raw materials. A decision has to be taken on maximum holdings, plans must be made to build up the stocks, records must be kept and control exercised to ensure the plan is fulfilled.

While these comments on the importance of stock control have been made in relation to the manufacturer, they are of course also relevant to the problems of the retailer. The shopkeeper has to try to keep enough stock to satisfy customers' demands while not carrying more stock than the business can finance. There are also other risks – for example, of deterioration of stock in the food shop or the risk of goods in the clothing shop becoming unfashionable.

In all these instances it is useful to set targets related to the annual rate of use, often stated as so many weeks' stock. For example, the average value of finished stock to be held is frequently stated as a percentage of annual sales value or as a corresponding number of weeks' sales. The level of raw material stocks may be stated in terms of a certain number of weeks' consumption in the workshop or factory.

Debtors

When, by effective control of stock and planning of production, the materials have moved through the process and become finished goods they will be sold to customers either immediately or from stock. The next step in reducing the overall time therefore will be to get payment from the customer immediately, or by the date specified in the conditions of sale. In most commercial transactions the time allowed is 30 days from the invoice date; but the business which can follow the example of the retailer and not allow credit avoids this problem altogether.

One way of reducing the size of the problem is to place a minimum order level on the value of goods which are to be supplied on credit. Apart from the saving in the time and paperwork involved in sending invoices, a considerable amount of time is saved which would otherwise have to be allocated to chasing debtors. Many companies adopt the practice for orders of low value or for new customers of sending out an advance invoice, known as a *pro-forma invoice*, before delivering the goods. The goods are then sent only on receipt of the cash.

When trading by credit is unavoidable (and in most manufacturing and several service industries this is so) a system should be devised to make the collection of debts a routine matter. Immediately the goods have been despatched or delivered, or the service job completed, an invoice should be submitted with request for payment within the agreed time. The practice of many firms whereby invoices are sent out at the end of the month, in effect gives the customer extra credit. The custom of sending monthly statements adds to the clerical work, but gives the customer a useful reminder not only of the current invoices but also those outstanding for earlier periods.

A record should be kept of all debtors showing the amounts outstanding and the length of time, if any, by which they are overdue. This is quite conveniently done by compiling from the personal ledgers a list in the form illustrated in Figure 8.2.

This list provides the information on which action can be taken in a systematic way. It appears in this example that V. Adams is probably being allowed too much time: perhaps the £400 worth of goods should not have been delivered until the outstanding amounts for the earlier months had been paid. T. Butler is not yet giving cause for alarm as the payment of £150 is only just due. G. Charles looks like one of the customers who places small orders but neglects to pay. Placing a minimum value of £20 for orders qualifying for credit could keep this customer off the list.

Figure 8.2

Customer	*Total*	*Age of debt*				
		Current	*1 month*	*2 months*	*3 months*	*3 months*
V. Adams	800	400	200	200	–	–
T. Butler	150	150	–	–	–	–
G. Charles	65	–	–	15	15	35

When reviewing this report the decision on what action to take will depend to a certain extent on the history of the firm's dealings with the customer. Sometimes a telephone call from owner to owner may be all that is needed. Frequently, the matter can be settled during a routine visit to the customer's buyer. But in general a routine somewhat on the following lines is desirable:

Prepare debtors list within one week of the end of each month.

Take appropriate action on all accounts overdue.

Seven days after the close of the month send by post a firm but polite reminder asking for payment within 7 days. If no reply is received within 7 days make a further request by telephone, or visit the person who is authorised to make payment. Then, if payment is not made immediately, stop any further deliveries.

After a further 2 weeks send a final letter, still polite, but pointing out that unless payment is made within 7 days it will be necessary to refer the matter to a third party for collection.

If payment is still withheld, refer the matter to the third party, e.g. a solicitor.

In most instances action on these lines usually results in payment being made. If it is not successful, a decision has to be taken whether or not to prosecute. In taking this decision the owner has to weigh up the cost of prosecuting against the likelihood of the result being favourable. The point to remember is that the longer that debts are outstanding the less likely it is that they will be paid, so the moral is to press for payment before it is too late. If the letter threatens legal action to recover the debt, then that threat must be carried out – otherwise do not make it.

In general it is probably more economical for a firm to establish a systematic procedure and to chase its own debtors than to employ outside agencies to do so. Claims up to £5000 may be pursued with a minimum of formality through the small claims procedure of the county court. In any event all claims up to £500 are referred by the court for arbitration without a formal court hearing.

There will however be many owners whose time is too valuable to spend on this activity. For these people it might be good practice to pass the debts to an agency for recovery of debts. The agency will, of course, charge a fee, but its experienced staff should be able to reduce the volume of bad debts and save the owner much valuable time.

Another method of bringing forward the receipt of cash is to factor or discount the invoices as soon as they are sent to customers. This means that copy invoices are passed to a factoring company (most banks have an associated company handling this work) which immediately pays an agreed proportion of the value of the invoice. The factoring company then proceeds to collect the full amount from the customer and pays the balance (less an agreed percentage) to the client. Although it might appear to be expensive, this service might be valuable to firms which have no staff to chase debtors, but which need cash early.

Many small firms are reluctant to take strong action against large customers for fear of losing their business; and some large firms take advantage of this fact and delay payment far beyond the stipulated date. Instances have occurred where reputable large manufacturing companies have owed cash to their small suppliers for nine or more months. Usually this reluctance is ill-judged. The well-managed small firm which meets its delivery dates with good quality work at the right (not necessarily the lowest) price rarely needs fear losing an order through pressing for payment. On the contrary, several small firms supplying large companies have found that a threat to stop future supplies has brought prompt payment. It need not always reach this stage. Frequently, a visit or even a telephone call to the person who authorises cheques – perhaps the chief accountant or the managing director – and an explanation of the difficulties caused by failure to pay will have the desired effect. The persistent claimant is often the one who gets paid first.

A discussion on credit control is not complete without some reference to discounts for prompt payment. It may seem attractive to be able to bring forward payment by perhaps a month by offering, say, 2½ per cent for prompt settlement. In a minority of cases when firms have been really desperate for cash to remain solvent, it has been worthwhile. It is not to be recommended as standard practice. Earlier we pointed out that it was probably right to take such discounts when offered because they represent a very high rate of interest. For the same reason it is usually not sensible to give discounts of this order. There is a further reason for not offering discounts for quick settlement: many customers will deduct the discount when paying the bill even when the payment is not made until well after the due date. The small firm usually finds that the cost of recovering this sum is not warranted by the amount recovered.

The Cash Forecast and Statement

In completing the cycle of working capital we have only dealt with the operating aspects of controlling cash so far. There are other payments to be made – perhaps the potter needs a new kiln, the roof repairer needs a new van, or the manufacturer needs a new machine. To plan expenditure on these fixed assets as well as on the working capital all these payments should be assembled in a *cash flow forecast*. (A simple form is illustrated in Figure 3.5.)

It may be that when this document is drawn up the negative cash balance for some months will not be acceptable. It might, for example, be necessary to postpone some of the expenditure on fixed assets, or negotiate extended payments. When it has been completed it can then become the plan against which progress can be monitored. In other words it is the cash budget and can be redesigned with columns to allow for actual results to be recorded. Figure 8.3 illustrates a more detailed cash flow forecast.

In this example the opening balance of cash at the bank (or the overdraft level) has been entered to enable an assessment to be made of what the bank statement should look like at the close of each month. It may be more realistic for certain businesses to prepare the cash flow forecast for say only four months ahead – January, February, March and April, and when January has ended to add the month of May to the forecast, and so on throughout the year.

In the first few weeks or months of a new venture there may be no revenues apart from the injection of capital, but there will be expenditure for the acquisition of premises, plant, stocks, etc., all of which should be carefully scheduled on the cash flow forecast.

Keeping the Balance

The firm which plans and controls its use of cash by the simple but

Figure 8.3

	January	February	March	April	May	June	November	December	Total
Sales	12 000	15 000	14 000	17 000	20 000	19 000	21 000	20 000	175 000
Other income	500			500					2 000
Total	12 500	15 000	14 000	17 500	20 000	19 000	21 000	20 000	177 000
Materials	5 000	4 000	6 000	5 000	6 000	7 000	6 000	7 000	61 500
Labour	5 000	4 000	4 000	5 000	4 000	4 000	4 000	5 000	52 500
Repairs	200	100	300	200	400	100	200	100	1 800
Power	300	200	200	300	200	200	200	300	2 400
Commission	130	150	160	140	160	180	150	180	1 900
Carriage	140	130	150	120	140	130	160	170	2 000
Packing material	300	200	–	–	250	100	300	200	1 800
Salaries	2 350	2 350	2 350	2 350	2 350	2 350	2 350	2 350	28 200
Water				50			50		100
Rates				1 250			1 250		2 500
Tools			100			50		70	300
Telephone & postage	20	30	250	20	10	20	20	200	800
Stationery		40		20	20	10	40	50	400
Interest						700		500	1 200
Insurances				1 300					1 300
Professional charges			450						450
Advertising	100	100	100	150	100	100	100	250	1 200
Travel & expenses	60	70	60	80	50	60	80	50	800
VAT	3 000			4 000					15 000
Total	16 600	11 370	14 120	19 980	13 680	15 000	14 900	16 320	175 650
Cash flow	(4 100)*	3 630	(120)*	(2 480)*	6 320	4 000	6 100	3 680	1 350
Balance at bank or overdraft ( )*	(4 800)*								(4 800)*
Cumulative cash flow	(8 900)*	(5 270)*	(5 390)*	(7 870)*	(1 550)*	2 450	(7 130)*	(3 450)*	(3 450)*

*Net outflows of cash.

effective means outlined in this chapter will be able to avoid two of the main causes of failure of many companies, large and small. It will ensure that early warning will be received of a threat to its solvency by watching that inflows of cash are available to meet the cash demands which will be made. It will be able to avoid the business sin of over-trading. This happens when the business expands at such a rate that the cash required to finance the expansion – for extra materials, labour, machines, premises – cannot be met by current sales revenue. This can happen even when the business is executing profitable orders.

Each owner should think carefully about his own business, and work out a system of cash control which fits the particular circumstances of the business. In this, as in other activities, there is no one system which fits all needs.

Security

Whatever systems or procedures the owner decides to instal they should operate against a background of close security of all cash and cheques. No cash expenditure should be allowed without proper authorisation, and receipt or vouchers must be produced for each purchase. Money should only be handled by the owner or a trusted assistant. Postage stamps should be strictly accounted for. (If the firm uses a large number of stamps a franking machine may be worth installing.) Finally, cheques should always require the signature of the owner or other partner or director and they should never be signed before the name of the payee and the amount of the cheque has been entered. These precautions may seem so obvious as not to warrant mention. However many small (and some larger) firms have lost large sums through failure to observe them.

9 Costs and Prices

Earlier chapters dealt with the question of selling prices, and considered the control of various costs in order to achieve a planned profit. Now we shall study a different aspect of cost – the cost of making the individual product or providing the service, and the relevance of these costs to the process of establishing the selling price. When considering price-setting in the context of the marketing activity, the point was made that the price which may be charged is that which the customer is prepared to pay. However, if the sale of the product or service is to make a profit, the price must clearly be high enough to cover the total cost and leave a surplus. It is obviously not possible to decide on this price without knowing how much the product or service will cost, so a method is needed of estimating in advance the probable costs that will be incurred. When the goods have been made or the service provided then it is necessary to know what costs have actually been incurred. These two aspects are usually referred to as *cost estimating* (before the work is started) and *cost determination* (after the work is finished). Before proceeding further it is important to bear in mind that when the estimate of cost has been made it is only one of several factors in deciding the selling price. The seller's judgement has a large part to play.

Costing

The process of cost estimating usually relies on experience gained from past operations. In the well-managed firm the necessary information will be drawn from financial records, so this aspect will be dealt with first.

It is usually fairly easy to collect the direct costs of making goods or providing a service. For example, a manufacturer of clothing would make out a job card for a batch of garments and record on this card the number of hours worked by each employee producing the goods, and also details of the materials used. Similarly, a painter and decorator could record the hours spent on each job, and the cost of paint, wallpaper, etc. used. The problem arises when an attempt is made to allow for the other costs of the business (to which the term overhead is usually applied) – rent, rates, telephone, heating, lighting, etc. – which are not directly related to the actual production of the goods or service.

Traditionally, it has been the practice in many small companies to deal with the problem by simply adding a percentage to the cost of labour and materials (often referred to as the *prime cost*) to allow for the overhead expenses. To show how the calculation is made we may refer back to the trading and profit and loss account (Figure 6.1). An analysis of the account produces the following figures:

Sales revenue	160 000
Direct cost, wages and materials	96 000
Overheads	49 000
Net profit	15 000

It will be seen from this that in the year to which the account refers, the figure for overheads was 51 per cent of the direct cost. The traditional method of costing has used this percentage in arriving at what was considered to be the total cost of a particular job or batch of work. The following example for the costs of a batch of product illustrate the technique:

	£
Materials	200
Labour	100
Total	300
51% of £300 for overheads	153
Total cost	453

Thus if its selling price is £500 the batch of work appears to have yielded a profit of £47.

Many owners who have conscientiously kept records of the costs of job or batches of work in this way have been disappointed to find at the end of the year that the firm has made only a very small profit – or even a loss – although every individual job appeared to have made a profit. What is the explanation? There are two common reasons either of which might give the answer: (i) The volume of business might have been less than adequate to provide the required profit even if every job had in fact been profitable. This cause should not be too difficult to identify as the astute owner should have recognised the lower level of activity. (ii) The mixture of work undertaken might have been different from that undertaken in the past. If the firm makes a range of products, or provides a range of services, a change in the proportion of each product or service to the total could cause the previous percentage addition to become invalid.

To illustrate the point assume the company is a ceramics company which makes only two products, A and B. Let us assume that the direct costs of a batch of each of the products are:

	A	*B*
Materials	100	50
Labour	50	100
Total direct cost	150	150
add 51% for overheads	76.5	76.5
Total cost	226.5	226.5
If the selling price is	300	300
The apparent profit is	73.5	73.5

Now although the total costs are apparently the same, it is possible that if, say, the sales of B increased substantially and A decreased by a similar amount, the actual overhead expenditure could change. This might arise because B requires a greater use of machinery than A does, or if product A is more bulky than product B it might need a longer time in the kiln leading to an increased consumption of gas. Whatever the final analysis, it would be a coincidence if the percentage to be added with the new mix of sales were the same as previously.

This change of mix might have come about gradually and for that reason it would be more difficult to recognise. The owner who had also maintained a monthly operating statement would, of course, have had an idea that the business was not on course, but the reason might not have been so clear.

There is an alternative which helps to avoid the dangers inherent in the traditional approach. It depends on the contribution concept already discussed in relation to the operating statement (see Figure 6.3). This method makes no attempt to establish the total cost of any product or service contract. Instead, the emphasis is placed on what each batch of product or each job contributes towards the fixed costs of the business and to profit, after the variable costs have been met. Looking again at the simple example of the ceramics firm, if the variable costs (other than labour and materials) for a batch of products A and B are A = £10 and B = £30, then the contribution made by a batch of A and a batch of B would be calculated thus:

			A	*B*
Selling price			300	300
Less variable costs				
Materials	100	50		
Labour	50	100		
Other variables	10	30		
			160	180
Contribution to fixed costs and profit			140	120

This indicates that a batch of product A contributes more than a batch of B. However, this does not necessarily mean that product A should be made at the expense of product B. It depends on how many batches of A could be made in a give period of time compared with the number of batches of B which could be made over a similar period. This brings us to the other important concept of the contribution approach – that of the *limiting factor*. If the workforce of the ceramics firm consists of the owner and a number of assistants the amount of work which the firm can produce in any given period may well depend on the number of hours they could in total devote to making the product. In other words, the factor which limited their output would be the number of man hours available. So the assessment of which product is more profitable could depend on the number of man hours which have to be spent on a batch of each product. If the man hours are Product A = 25 and Product B = 50 then the contribution per man hour of batches of the respective products would be:

Product A £140 ÷ 25 = £5.60
Product B £120 ÷ 50 = £2.40

But supposing the limiting factor were not the available man hours, but instead the total output were limited by the capacity of the kiln. Then the more profitable product would be the one which yielded a higher contribution per kiln hour. Assume that the kiln hours per batch are Product A = 15 and Product B = 10, then the contribution per kiln hour would be:

Product A £140 ÷ 15 = £9.33
Product B £120 ÷ 10 = 12.0

The relative profitability in these circumstances has changed quite substantially. This illustrates the importance of identifying the factor which limits the total output before making any assumptions about profitability.

However, we have still not answered the all-important question: Is the profit enough to meet the firm's profit target? This is now a relatively simple matter. Taking first the assumption that the limiting factor is the number of man hours available, let us assume that in a year the number of effective hours available is 16,000. Then, if the only product made were A, the annual contribution would be 16,000 × £5.60 = £89,600. If only product B were made the annual contribution would be 16,000 × £2.4 =38,400. If half the hours were spent on each product the total contribution would be 8000 × £5.60 + 8000 × £2.4 = £64,000. The calculation for other sales proportions of A and B can be made similarly. It now remains to subtract the budgeted fixed costs from the contribution provided by the chosen mix of products to establish the probable annual profit, and to compare this with the target.

A similar calculation would be made if it were decided that the limiting factor was the output per kiln hour.

Needless to say, the profit will be achieved only if the required effective number of man hours or kiln hours are realised in practice. This means that a record must also be kept of the number of these hours which are fully employed.

Cost Estimating and Price-fixing

So far we have studied the costing process in a firm which has compiled a record of costs from practical experience. The discussion might appear to be irrelevant to the new firm starting out with no records to guide it. However, the owner who intends to manage the firm effectively will have set a profit target for the first year, have estimated the fixed costs, and will have made a rough estimate – perhaps based on experience as an employee in a similar business –

of the variable costs involved in making the product or supplying the service.

This means that there is enough information available to determine the minimum selling price for a batch of work which would enable the firm to reach its profit target. The procedure is in effect the reverse of the costing process, and in outline is as follows:

Calculate the required annual contribution (fixed costs plus target profit).
Identify the limiting factor – assumed for this example to be the number of man hours available.

Calculate the required contribution per man hour

$$\frac{\text{total contribution}}{\text{effective hours available}}$$

Estimate the variable costs incurred in providing the product/service (materials, labour, carriage, etc.).
Estimate the number of man hours needed to make the batch of the product or provide the service.
Multiply the number of man hours by the required contribution per man hour.
Add this figure to the total variable cost.

The result is the target selling price.

When this approach to price-setting is adopted other advantages accrue. It may, for example, occur from time to time that the target selling price is not achievable – perhaps during an economic recession prices are being depressed by competitors anxious to get the work. When this happens, it is possible to assess the amount by which prices may be reduced before a danger-point is reached. It will obviously be unwise ever to sell a product or service at below the variable cost – this would mean that every sale made would decrease the annual profit, or add to the annual loss.

There are other reasons why it may be advisable to reduce prices temporarily below the target price. An example is provided by business is whose work tends to be seasonal. The proprietor of a small hotel might find business slack during the winter when the holiday/tourist trade is finished. He may decide to accept guests during this off-season at prices below that normally charged in the high season. Possibly in this case he would calculate on a lower contribution, to cover all variable costs and a small contribution toward the fixed costs. During the busy season he should obviously try to get higher prices than the target price in order to compensate for the lower contribution during the slack season.

The examples in this chapter have deliberately been taken from manufacturing or service industries, because it is in these firms that the advantages of using the contribution concept are most pronounced. The retailer has a rather less complicated problem to solve, as practically all the variable costs consist of the goods purchased for re-sale. Otherwise the costs are largely fixed. The aim here therefore must be to buy at the most favourable prices and to select the selling price which customers will pay without losing the volume necessary to meet the fixed costs in the longer term. These prices may be those recommended by the manufacturers (RRP) or such prices as the customers are prepared to pay. These are matters calling for skill, judgement and experience. Even so, in some businesses the concepts might be useful – for example, if space is at a premium it may be a sound policy to stock only those items where the contribution per square metre is above a certain figure. Most small retailers however fnd that the limiting factor is the volume of sales. When this is so the aim will be to get a level of contribution per £ of sales from the mix of products sold which will, in total, achieve the annual target profit.

10 Financial Planning

The information contained in the financial statements discussed so far, while satisfying some of the obligations, is nevertheless historic. For this reason some positive attempt should be made to forecast the revenues and expenditure to be incurred in, say, the year ahead. These forecasts are termed *budgets* and may be set out in the same simple format as a trading and profit and loss account, or in a much more detailed manner. The purpose of these budgets is to provide a basis against which actual performances can be monitored, and allow management to take corrective action on those items which show unacceptable variations from the budgets. The fact that the business is looking ahead of itself is a good thing because it requires the whole business strategy to be considered.

The normal practice is to compare the actual expenditure and revenues against budget monthly, but it may be appropriate to make the comparison quarterly or on a seasonal basis. It is also customary not only to show the period under review but the cumulative results for the year to date.

A procedure for setting as a simple system of budgets may be demonstrated by referring back to the company whose profit and loss accounts and balance sheet were discussed in chapters 6 and 7.

It is a useful first step to set a profit target for the business. The owner of a business will expect the business to make a higher profit than would be achieved by investing the same capital in the bank, building society or other safe venture. The extra profit is justified by the extra risk inherent in running one's own business, and probably the minimum return looked for would be at least 25 per cent of the capital invested in the firm.

Having set the target for profit, the necessary sales revenue can be determined by reference to the profit graph in Figure 6.4, p. 88. Let us assume that the owner has set a target of 30 per cent return on the capital employed, so that the actual target for profit is £22,500 (30 per cent of £75,000). It wil be seen from the graph that this profit will be achieved at a level of sales of £182,000 against total costs of £159,500.

If market research indicates that this sales revenue is realistic with the given order mix, the next step is to make plans to achieve the necessary sales. This will involve setting target levels for each product or service, probably varying from month to month to allow for seasonal variations.

It will next be necessary to assess the action to be taken to provide the goods or services required to meet the sales demand. This will involve calculations as to type and quantities of materials, number of employees, types of machines, and all the other items and activities associated with providing the products or services. These various numbers and quantities are then converted to money values, which provide the raw material of the resulting budgets. However, before developing the final budgets a check must be made that the relationships between costs and revenue have not changed significantly. This means in the example chosen that the fixed costs are unchanged at £40,800 and that variable costs are in the region of £118,700 (£159,500 total costs less £40,800 fixed costs).

These calculations lead to the construction of the annual budget, giving details of all sales revenue and the costs associated with achieving those sales. However, if progress against the budget is to be monitored it will be necessary to check at frequent and regular inteverals during the year what revenue has been generated and what costs incurred. This is usually done by developing monthly budgets from the annual budget. We have already mentioned the probability of the pattern of sales varying from month to month because of seasonal factors. It is almost certain that the volume of production of goods or services will also vary from month to month, not only because of seasonal factors, but also because there are different numbers of working days in different months, and because allowances have to be made for holidays. Thus each month will have its own distinctive budget and the total of all these budgets will agree with the annual budget.

These monthly budgets are usually set out in a similar manner to the operating statement referred to in Figure 6.3, but expanded to show:

Budget for the period.
Actual results for the period.
Cumulative budget since the beginning of the year.
Cumulative results since the beginning of the year.

A statement for the month of May for the same company would be presented as shown in Figure 10.1 (The term *variance* means the variation from the budget.)

Figure 10.1

Operating Statement X May 1982 (19 working days)

	Budget	*Actual*	*Variance*
Sales	15 000	16 000	1 000+
Direct & variable costs			
Materials	4 800	5 200	400–
Labour	3 900	4 100	200–
Repairs	170	150	20+
Power	195	200	5–
Commission	185	200	15–
Carriage	150	160	10–
Packing	80	80	–
Total	9 480	10 090	610–
Contribution	5 520	5 910	390
Fixed costs			
Production*	1 600	1 590	10+
Administration*	1 700	1 800	100–
Selling & distribution*	200	150	50+
Total	3 500	3 540	40–
Operating profits	2 020	2 370	350+

* The individual items included under these headings may be detailed on the statement or in supporting notes.
\+ Saving or gain over budget.
– Overspend or loss over budget.

As indicated, it may not be necessary to report in detail all the fixed costs every month. Maintenance of these statements as far down as the contribution line will, in many cases, be adequate to give the owner the confidence of knowing the business in on course.

For people who prefer to deal with diagrams rather than figures, the profit graph may seem an alternative means of recording progress against budget. This is true, but it is not possible to put as much detail in the chart as in a full statement. Many owner-managers do in fact draw up a profit graph at the beginning of the year and display it on a wall-board in the office. Then month by month the cumulative sales revenue is plotted on the chart, indicating when the break-even point for the year's trading has been reached.

However, if this is done it is essential that the total variable and fixed costs are also plotted month by month so that any change in the relationship between sales revenue, variable costs and fixed costs can be quickly identified. Firms have gone out of business through watching the sales line while ignoring the cost lines.

The final step in setting up the system of budgets is to develop the budget for the cash to finance the expenditure entailed in all the operations reported upon in the operating statement. This has already been described in chapter 8 and illustrated in Figure 8.3. It should be noted that the revenue and expenditure which are forecast and recorded in the cash statement will not coincide with those in the operating statement for the same month. This is because payment for goods or services invoiced in one month may not be received until perhaps two months later. Similarly payments for many of the good and services purchased by the firm will also be delayed and paid for in a later month.

The procedures described in this chapter have been illustrated by examples from small manufacturing industry. Almost identical practices would be appropriate to the firm offering a service. The retailer would not require such detailed procedures and accounts but the underlying principles still apply.

Budgeting for the New Venture

The examples used in this chapter have used the accounts of a business which has been operating for at least a year in order to have figures to work to. How does all this concern the new venture, and what relevance does this have to the process of starting up? The answer is that although it has been convenient for ease of illustration to look at an existing business, exactly the same principles apply to the thinking necessary before starting to trade. In earlier chapters reference has been made to the need for the owner to set clear objectives for the business, and to carry out the research necessary to ensure that the objectives could be met. Also emphasised was the need to do exactly this kind of preparation to convince bank managers and other possible backers of the soundness of the venture.

Thus although the calculations for the new venture must of necessity be made without a sound base of fact, nevertheless enough information will have been assembled to plan ahead with a reasonable degree of confidence.

In case any readers might still feel that all this is too much for the new firm to tackle, let us return to the example in chapter 1 of the three people who set up a new small textile firm in a very competitive market. After thorough research these people decided that there was a small part of the market which was not being adequately catered for. They assessed the amount of capital required, estimated the operating costs, and calculated the profit available from their anticipated market. This proved to be in line with their ideas, so they planned the venture. Before starting the manufacturing of the product they produced a budget for the first year and tentative plans for the next three years. Then the first years' budget was analysed into twelve monthly operating statements and cash budgets almost exactly as described in this chapter.

As the first year progressed the actual performance of the firm almost exactly coincided with the budget; when there were any variations they were very quick to take remedial action. At the end of the first year the profit target had been achieved. Finally, at the end of the third year, their results were even better than had been planned. The owners were all perfectly satisfied that without all this preliminary thought and work, the stimulus of working to a target, and the guidance provided by their monthly statements, the achievement of the firm would have been very much less satisfactory.

11 Planning Operations

The Need for Planning

Most people at one time or another have had the unhappy experience of being let down by a supplier when they have bought, or tried to buy, goods or services from a retailer, tradesman or manufacturer.

Perhaps we have been to the shop where we usually buy some commodity only to find the product is out of stock. Or we might have given the local builder an order to modernise the bathroom and put in a new window. The work has started, holes have been knocked in walls, and then the work has stopped for several days or weeks because materials have not arrived. The electrician is too busy elsewhere at just the time he is required to rewire the room. Or perhaps we have ordered carpets to a particular design to be supplied and fitted in our new house by the local furnishing shop and the owner of the shop had promised that the work would be completed by our date for moving in. The quoted date was based on the delivery date quoted by the manufacturer; however the manufacturer failed to deliver and our arrangements had to be revised.

In very many cases of this nature the failure to meet the customers' wishes has been due to a lack of control of operations arising from a lack of adequate planning by the supplier or manufacturer.

Consider the three examples. If the shopkeeper had planned the type and quantity of goods to be held in stock and had placed orders for replacements in good time it is unlikely that the goods would not have been available. (There will, of course, be occasions when some happening outside the control of the shopkeeper will hold up delivery.)

If the builder had carefully planned the job, the estimate he gave for the completion date would have been more reliable. The materials would have been ordered in good time, and the electrician would have been booked for the days when his services would be needed. The builder would have kept in touch with the suppliers of materials to ensure they kept to the planned dates. If it appeared that there would be a hold-up in the supply of materials the plan could have been changed so that work once started could be carried through continuously to completion.

Similarly the carpet manufacturer (possibly quite a small company) would probably not have let the furnishing shop down if supplies of materials, the use of looms, and the time of the operators had been planned and co-ordinated to meet the requirements of the various customers.

It follows that if the new venture is to succeed, this matter of planning and controlling the operations of the company must have a very high priority in the proprietor's thinking, for as these examples show, one of the key features of good service is completion of the service or delivery of the goods by the promised date. A simple plan made before work starts will provide the guide which the owner needs to ensure that all action taken is directed towards meeting that date. Equally important, if any deviation from the plan occurs it can be detected, and corrective action taken in good time.

There is another very good reason for planning: a sound plan followed conscientiously leads to reduced costs. First, the person responsible for buying materials (probably the owner) will be able to defer the delivery until they are actually required, thus savng the cost of the money which would otherwise be tied up in materials lying idle in the store. Secondly, there is a better chance that work once started will continue smoothly through to the finish, avoiding the extra cost incurred through cash being tied up in work which cannot be completed. Thirdly, when more than one person is involved in the work, a sound plan will keep to a minimum the times when one person has to wait for the others. This is especially important in the building industry where many different trades are involved – carpenters, bricklayers, plasterers, electricians, etc. Here the time lost through tradesmen waiting for each to finish his part of the work can lead to heavy and unnecessary extra costs.

In this chapter some simple techniques of planning and control are reviewed. They will be especially appropriate to the manufacturer and to the business offering a service. While they are less relevant to the needs of the retailer, the principles involved may be of interest, particularly if a service is being offered as part of the retail operation. We shall look first at the planning and control of operations, and then turn our attention to the question of stock control.

Planning Operations

In any business it may just be possible to survive in the early days with no formal planning and with control relying very much on the owner's memory. However, in all manufacturing firms and most service businesses a time is almost certain to come when a more formal approach is essential if the business is to operate effectively. Unfortunately the smaller firm only too often fails to recognise the need for more formal planning until the business is getting out of control and its reputation marred. Typical 'symptoms' when this stage is reached are an excessive amount of unfinished work; late deliveries to customers (or late completion of the service contract); and increasing costs.

The degree of planning required to avoid these undesirable results need not call for complicated systems or reams of paperwork. But the owner of even the smallest enterprise must accept that some paperwork is necessary, and from the start should devise a procedure and system to suit the business. It is important that when a suitable system has been developed it is adhered to unless there are extremely good reasons for departing from it. In other words discipline is essential.

There are two aspects of planning which should be considered when procedures are being developed. First, there is the need to plan and control the work so that the specified delivery date or completion date will be met. Secondly, there is the need to use machines, equipment, materials and employees' time effectively so that costs are kept within the budget. Often there is conflict between these two needs. For example, in order to meet a delivery date it might be necessary to buy a more expensive material because cheaper material, though of adequate quality, is temporarily out of stock, or it might be necessary to employ people on overtime, at extra cost, to make up for time unavoidably lost. This means that planning cannot be a completely mechanical process and that the owner's or manager's judgement will always be an important factor.

In essence the planning of the day-to-day work of the business is very simple. There are only three steps:

(1) For each job, work out the sequence of operations and then estimate the length of time needed to complete each operation.
(2) Working back from the required delivery date, calculate the date by which each operation has to be started for the completion date to be met.

(3) Place orders for materials or sub-contract services to be available at the required starting date.

In practice it is not quite so simple, especially when several jobs are in hand at the same time. In planning job A, the services of certain employees or machines will have been reserved for definite periods of time. Now when job B is being planned it may well be that one or more of these employees or machines is required at the same time. To prevent this a record must be kept of all times thus allocated for all the jobs being executed. This record must be consulted before completion dates are agreed so that the person making the commitment can be reasonably certain of its being kept.

This record, usually referred to as the *loading record* or *loading chart*, also helps to meet the second requirement – that the resources available to the firm are used effectively. A study of the record will show which resources are lightly loaded and which tend to be overloaded, thus offering guidance as to any corrective action required.

It is instructive to see how these principles can be applied in different types of business. The simplest form of planning is probably that practised by a professional such as a hairstylist working on his own. This person usually keeps a diary in which appointments are entered as they are made. The act of writing in each appointment creates, in effect, a loading record because the hairstylist knows from experience the length of time to be devoted to each client. Each hour is thus loaded with an appropriate quantity of work. Both of the requirements of good planning have been met because the customer will have the work done by the promised time, and the hairstylist's time will be used effectively.

Consider now the electrician who undertakes contracts for installation of electrical services in homes or industrial premises. Here there is a slightly more complicated problem, and planning requires more forethought. Before a contract can be obtained the premises have to be surveyed, so that a quotation can be prepared for the customer stating the date by which the work could be completed and the price to be charged for the work. This delivery date is estimated after account has been taken of several factors, including:

The load already placed on the business by other jobs in hand.
The delivery time required for the delivery of material.
The number of hours of work required after receipt of materials.
Dates on which access to the premises is possible.

In making these calculations the electrician must bear in mind that he cannot spend all working hours doing practical work. Some time must be set aside (perhaps one half day or one day a week) for attending to the commercial activities of the business and marketing the service, otherwise the time might come when there are no orders on the books, and hence no continuity of work.

Although the electrician's problem is more complicated than the hairstylist's, his planning could still be a simple process. All that is needed is a diary in which are recorded the dates on which materials are ordered, when they are due in, how long each job should take, the date when each job has to start and when it has to be finished. This diary is thus both the planning document and the control document, used for working out when various activities should occur, for checking whether dates are being kept, and for keeping a record of the load of work on the business.

In the manufacturing or service business which has employees, the process becomes more complicated and more formalised procedures and documents are necessary.

One device very widely used in planning operations in businesses of all sizes is the *bar chart*, where a line or bar is drawn to scale to represent the time any particular operation will take. Figure 11.1 indicates the kind of chart which might be suitable for the electrical contractor in the service business. (*a*) illustrates the dates on or by which various operations in each contract are carried out; (*b*) shows how the time of members of staff is allocated to different contracts.

To study the methods which may be used in the manufacturing company let us consider a company producing clothing from materials which have to pass through several bench and machine operations before completion. The example has been deliberately simplified to make the principle clearer. Certain information is essential before the planning process can start:

The operations which are necessary in making the garments.
The date by which the customer wants the goods.
The time which the factory or workshop has already committed to existing orders.
The availability of materials.

Having estabished this information, the next step is to draw up a sheet listing all operations necessary, and an estimate of the time each one will take. A typical lay-out illustrated in Figure 11.2
At the same time a list of the materials must be drawn up. Figure 11.3 illustrates a typical lay-out.

Figure 11.1
(a) operation dates

Customer	*Job no.*	*Week ending* 15 April	22 April	30 April	7 May	14 May
W. Jones Ltd	158	Materials on order		Wire Mains	Connect Machine	Test Run
C. Smith Ltd	159	Materials on order		Fit Power Points		Instal Equipment

(b) Staff allocation

Work to be done by:	*Week ending:* *15 April*	*22 April*	*30 April*	*7 May*	*14 May*
Owner	Job 152		Job 158		Job 159
S. Brown	Job 152	Job 156	Job 159		Job 158

With this information the customer's order can be planned by starting from the required delivery date and working back through all operations so assessing when each operation must start and finish and when material must be made available. The starting and finishing dates can be indicated by adding two columns to the list of operations, as shown in Figure 11.4

The next step is to book the times required for the various operations on a set of loading charts (one for each machine or process) which can be laid out as in Figure 11.5 or on a bar chart as in Figure 11.6

Although this example illustrates the planning process in a workshop, the same techniques can be supplied in service industry. The builder, for example, may see a similarity between his business and the manufacturing firm. Instead of marking-out tables and machines we can substitute bricklayers, carpenters, plumbers, etc, and the loading charts for the various trades can be similar to that for Machine B.

Figure 11.2

Job no. P83			
Operation *No.*	*Detail*	*Machine, etc.*	*Estimated time*
1	Mark out	Marking-out table	10 hours
2	Cut out	Cutting table	20 hours
3	Machine	Machine B	15 hours
4, 5	(Further operations as necessary)		

Figure 11.3

Job no. P83

Component	*Quantity*	*Material*	*Quantity per garment*	*Total Quantity*

Figure 11.4

Job no. P83

Operation No.	*Detail*	*Machine or work section*	*Estimated time (hrs)*	*Start date*	*Finish date*
1	Mark out	marking out table	10	19 January	20 January
2	Cut out	cutting table	20	21 January	27 January
3	Machine	Machine B	15	29 January	2 February
4, 5, 6	(Further operations as necessary)				

Figure 11.5 *Load chart in tabular form (one chart per machine, bench or type of skill*

Machine B (Machine hours available =32)									
Week ending									
15 January			22 January			29 January			5 February
Job	*Hours*	*Total hours*	*Job*	*Hours*	*Total hours*	*Job*	*Hours*	*Total hours*	*etc.*
P52	10	10	P81 (continued)	14	14				
P54	15	25							
P81	7	32		(etc.)			(etc.)		(etc.)

Figure 11.6 *Bar chart including all machines, etc. on one chart*

	Week ending			
Machine or bench	*15 January*	*22 January*	*29 January*	*5 February*
Machine B	P52 | P54	P81		
Marking-out table	(other machines, etc. planned similarly)			
Cutting table				

After some experience of planning in this way it often becomes evident that one or two machines in the workshop, or one or more trades in the service business, tend to be loaded more heavily than others, and thus tend to control the whole process. When this is the case, it is usually only necessary to keep loading records of these key machines or trades. The other operations are then fitted in at convenient times.

Carrying out the Work

Now that the work has been planned, it is necessary to get the job started at the right time, and to control its progress through the various operations. In all but the smallest of business it is advisable to use some kind of document to assist in this process.

If the owner is operating in a businesslike way, whether as sole trader, partnership, or limited company, an official written order will have been obtained from the customer before work starts. This applies not only to the manufacturing firm but also to the electrician, carpenter or any other business providing a service which calls for the use of materials of high value or involving many manhours. In the early days this order may be adequate to provide all the information necessary to plan, carry out and control the work. At a very early stage however it is advisable to initiate internal order forms. Each order from a customer is allocated a serial number from a register. An internal order carrying this number is then prepared translating the customer's order into terms familiar to the people concerned with planning and carrying out the work. The issue of this document is the signal for work to start. As the job proceeds through its operations it is identified by this number, and any documents relating to cost, material purchases, despatch and invoicing carry the same number. This makes it easier to identify work in progress, to collect information relating to the order, and to control operations.

Although we have suggested that this practice is necessary as the business begins to grow, in many enterprises the owner has set up and followed a simple system along these lines even before the business has received its first order. This has paid off because the discipline practised from the start has enabled the business to develop in an orderly manner.

To sum up, it is essential for any person starting out in business to think carefully about how the work is to be controlled and make sure that the following steps are taken at an early stage.

Create a simple system of documents to ensure that customers' requirements are made clear to all concerned in the firm.

Plan work and adopt procedures to ensure that:

- Delivery promises are kept;
- work in progress is limited to that necessary to meet customers' needs;
- employees and machines in the firm have a load of work as regular and even as orders permit;

the progress of work from the office through to despatch can be readily checked; and

materials arrive before work is due to start, but not so early as to incur high costs in carrying stock for long periods.

Quality

One aspect which must always be borne in mind is that all plans and procedures will be of no avail if the quality of the work does not meet customers' needs. At the outset the owner of the new business must decide the quality standards to be aimed for, and take steps to see they are maintained. It is often forgotten that quality of service has to be maintained as well as quality of product. The quality of the professional person will be measured not only by the adequacy of the professional service but also by the promptness and helpfulness with which clients' needs are met. The quality of the electrician's or plumber's work is measured not only by the excellence of the wiring or the plumbing, but also by the state in which the site is left and by the promptness with which the work is completed. The shopkeeper will ensure that the quality of goods offered meets the claims made for them; but as well as this, the quality of the small retailer's service will also be judged by his knowledge of the product and ability to offer specialist advice. The manufacturer making a finished product for sale to the public will have set a standard to meet the needs of the market which the firm sets out to satisfy. This means establishing the right quality for that market. If quality is too low the product will not sell; if too high, unnecessary costs are incurred, making the product unprofitable at a price which customers are prepared to pay.

The firm carrying out work under sub-contract for a larger company will have its standards set by that company. It must take steps to ensure that its practices, equipment, training of employees and procedures for inspecting work are geared to meeting those standards.

Thus all businesses, however small, must establish standards of quality of product and service, make the necessary arrangements to meet that quality, and set up a checking procedure to ensure customers' needs are met.

Control of Stock

Closely allied to control of the activities of people and machines is the control of stock. This aspect is of vital importance to the retailer. If the shop carries too little stock it loses customers. If it carries too much, there is too much money and space tied up in stock and there is increased risk of goods becoming out of date or deteriorating. By analysing past sales the shopkeeper must use his judgement in setting maximum and minimum levels of stock for each item, and must keep records of receipts and sales to check actual quantities in stock. Then orders have to be placed to ensure that stocks are replenished so that neither minimum nor maximum levels are reached. The owner of a service business has a slightly different problem. Consider a small firm operating a carpentry and joinery business. There will be the need to keep certain standard sizes of timber in stock which experience shows are likely to be needed frequently. The same applies to fittings, screws, etc. In principle the firm has a similar problem to that of the retailer, though paperwork and procedures will probably differ. An extra problem in this particular business is that a procedure is needed not only to record receipts and issues of timber, but also to record returns of material not used – off-cuts or part lengths.

In addition it will be difficult to assess what materials need to be kept in stock to meet the many and varied demands of individual customers, and a long period of trading may be necessary before a pattern can be established. Many businesses of this type have found themselves carrying too much, too little, or the wrong stock through failure to keep adequate records and make proper plans at the start of operations.

The manufacturer is even more in need of efficient procedures. This type of business will need to keep stocks of raw material adequate to keep work moving through the workshop. If the firm makes a finished product, then stocks of finished goods must also be kept ready for despatch to customers. Again the same principles apply: Set levels for minimum and maximum levels for each item; establish a procedure for re-ordering at the right time; and keep records to show the quantity of stock held.

When many different items of raw materials or finished goods are to be kept in stock it helps to keep a formal record based on a system of stock record cards. A typical card of the type used in many companies is illustrated in Figure 5.3, p. 56. Figure 11.7 shows a simpler form which may be suitable to some businesses, but each business will need to develop its own record to meet its particular needs. The form 'reorder level' calls for explanation. The figure inserted here represents the level to which stocks may be allowed to

Figure 11.7 *Stock Record Card*

Description:................... *Part No*...................
Location:................... Min. stock.................
Max. stock................
Re-order level............

Date	*Order on supplier*		*Received quantity*	*Issued quantity*	*Balance in stock*
	No.	*Quantity*			

fall without a serious risk of running out of stock before new supplies can be obtained. This is a matter for judgement by the owner after taking into account the reliability of suppliers in meeting their quoted delivery dates. It will be noted that when the firm is its own customer (i.e. making for stock) the re-order level must be set so that the factory or workshop has adequate time to meet the requirement.

Planning the Methods of Working

Any discussion on planning would be incomplete without some reference to working methods. Considerable savings of time can often be achieved by a study of the methods now in use, and the application of common sense. One fruitful source of saving is the lay-out of the equipment fixtures and machines. For example, even in the very small workshop it frequently happens that store shelves, machines and benches are laid out in a haphazard manner so that materials travel quite long distances moving through the sequence of operations. A little thought often results in a new lay-out in which this distance is considerably reduced. The ideal arrangement of course is where the equipment can be laid out in the same order as the sequence of operations.

When studying the actual methods used both in workshops and offices the owner may well take a leaf from the work-study specialist's book in these matters and ask the following questions about all the firm's operations:

What are we doing? . . . Why?
When is it done? . . . Why then?
Where is it done? . . . Why there?
Who is doing it? . . . Why that person?
How is it done? . . . Why?

A critical study using these questions may result in some quite significant improvements.

This chapter has covered varied aspects of control of the business and has given a brief indication of some of the techniques employed. It needs to be emphasised that each firm whether sole trader, partnership, or limited company is unique, and has unique problems to solve. It follows that detailed systems and practices which work well in one firm may fail dismally in another, so each owner or manager must work out procedures which suit his firm. Many proprietary systems are on the market. When the systems best suited to the firm have been developed one of these proprietary systems can perhaps be modified to suit. But the system must be adapted to the firm, not the firm to the system.

12 Managing People

When the business has reached the stage that people have to be employed, the owner or manager has the added task of managing people. The person who has had experience as a manager in a large company will probably have a fair idea of what is involved. Even so, he will find that managing people in the smaller unit is a different task from that in the large company. All the matters which may have been attended to by special departments or advisers have to be dealt with by the owner personally. Persons who come straight from a trade or profession in which they had no responsibilities for employees will meet difficulties which they had never before considered.

First of all there are legal requirements to be met. There will be national and local legislation covering safety, conditions of work and rights of employees. Then there might be organisations of labour to deal with. The very small firm usually has few problems here – often the people have joined the firm because they like the informality and freedom of the small unit, and prefer to settle difficulties directly with the boss.

This book will not deal at length with legal aspects. The prudent person will take steps to become familiar with, and to keep up with the changes to legislation, and also to locate a solicitor experienced in labour law to whom to turn when in doubt. (Chapter 13 summarises the matters covered by current national legislation and includes a list of Acts and Regulations.)

Neither shall we spend much time on how to negotiate with labour organisations. The well-managed small firm is unlikely to meet difficulties which call for formal intervention by unions. If it does appear that difficulties are arising the prudent owner-manager will join an employers' association which provides guidance and practical help in negotiations.

What we shall deal with is the task of managing people in such a way that they will put in the effort and use their mental and physical abilities to help the firm achieve its objectives.

At the outset it is important to realise that when the first employee is taken on the owner must delegate some part of his work to that person, otherwise there is no reason for employing anyone. This means that the owner has to be very clear on several points:

The reason why it became necessary to employ the person.
What work he is expected to do.
What responsibilities, if any, are to be placed on the person.
What authority, if any, is to be granted to the employee to meet the responsibilities.

Not only must the boss be clear on these points, but so must the employee. This means that the boss has the duty to make sure the employee fully understands the nature of the job. As the firm employs more people they must know not only details of their job, but also how their job fits into the overall pattern. They will need to know whom they are answerable to, and what are the jobs of other people whose work impinges on theirs.

All this takes a lot of thought and time, more than many entrepreneurs are prepared to devote to it. But time spent on these matters at the start will pay dividends by lightening the load on the boss, and reducing the number of queries or difficulties to be dealt with personally. Employees who know what is expected of them are more likely to maintain an interest in their work and to use their initiative in taking decisions. This does not mean that the boss loses control. Although many responsibilities will have been delegated, periodical checks will still be needed to ensure that the jobs are being done as intended, and that planned results are being achieved.

Without realising it the founder of a new business will, when engaging employees, have created a new social group. This can give rise to the difficulties and human problems which arise when a number of people group together for any purpose. So the leader of the group (the owner or manager) has to be constantly on the look out for warning signs of friction which may hamper the progress of the business towards its objectives. At the same time the effective leader will be looking at the positive side, blending compatible people into groups which can work well together. Again, this takes time which the keen owner would have preferred to spend on the technical or business side of operations.

Many specialists in the field of human relations – university academics, personnel managers and industrialists – have given much thought to these matters. Many theories have been advanced as to the means by which people may be induced or encouraged to put in the effort needed to do their job well. It is not the aim of this book to present these various theories of motivation (as the subject is called) but there are a few guidelines which are generally agreed to be reliable.

Some people appear to have some natural quality which enables them to get other people to work well and amicably. They achieve this with little apparent effort or forethought. If the process really is as effortless as it seems, these people are lucky. Others have to work harder to get the same result. How can this be achieved?

The process starts with the selection of employees, matching jobs to people and people to jobs. If the guidance given earlier in the chapter is followed, the manager will have thought out in detail why the new recruit is required. Responsibilities will have been clearly defined, and also the duties the person selected is expected to carry out. The authority which the job carries will have been defined. Also the relationship of this job to other jobs will have been made clear.

It is a useful discipline for the founder of the new company to write out a definition on these lines for each job which arises as the organisation develops. A simple lay-out is shown in Figure 12.1 but the individual owner will use whatever form suits the firm's needs.

The next step is to get a mental picture of the person who would ideally fit this job, and so we ask ourselves a few questions: What kind of person has the qualities needed to meet the responsibilities? What qualities are we looking for in a person who has authority to take decisions on our behalf? Are any special skills needed to carry out the tasks? What temperament is called for in dealing with other people in the firm, including ourselves? We are now in a position to look for a person who could meet the needs of the job and fit smoothly into the growing organisation. The process of building up this picture can be made more systematic by analysing, under suitable headings, the attributes we would expect to find in this person.

Some years ago the National Institute of Industrial Psychology in London developed their seven-point plan, which has since been used widely, and has stood the test of time. The headings used in this plan are:

Physical attributes	– health, strength, endurance, appearance, speech, manner, age.
Attainments	– education and training (general, technical, clerical, etc.) needed to meet the demands of the job.

	– experience gained in previous jobs which would be relevant to this job.
General intelligence	reasoning ability, quickness of understanding (remember that some jobs may be too boring for a person of high intelligence).
Special aptitudes	– facility with figures, ability to analyse problems, manual dexterity, etc.
Disposition	– reaction to events likely to occur in the job, e.g. is it likely the job would be done better by a careful phlegmatic person, or does it call for someone who prefers plenty of action?
Interests	– are there any interests outside work indicating a natural ability which would be useful in the job? On the other hand, are there any interests which would make a person less suitable (e.g. which would entail loss of time at busy periods)?
Circumstances	– the kind of background of the ideal person, e.g. how near to the firm must the person live? Is a married or single person more suitable?

If a procedure such as this is followed the chances of making a good selection are increased, and if it is necessary to advertise the job, this procedure will help in designing an advertisement to attract the right people too. If any agency (public or private) is used, they can be given a very clear idea of the person the firm is looking for. At the interview stage the clear definitions of the job and the ideal person will help the interviewer ask the applicant the right questions. The result will be that, at best, the ideal person will be found or, at worst, a bad misfit will be avoided.

In practice it is likely that the final choice will be less than ideal. It may be that the job will have to be modified to make best use of the strengths of the individual. This could mean that the boss may retain certain duties which he would prefer to delegate, while delegating other tasks and responsibilities which were intended to be retained. In other words, if the person is not an ideal fit in the job, the job might have to be made to fit the person.

Good selection lays the foundation for building a well-motivated staff. To build on this foundation we need pay attention to two essential aspects: administration and leadership.

Figure 12.1 *Job description*

Job title:

Purpose of job:

Accountable to: (who the job-holder answers to)

Subordinates: (who answers to the job holder)

Accountable for:

1.
2.
3.
4.
5.
6.

(details of key results the job-holder is expected to achieve)

Authority:

1.
2.
3.
4.

(details of the authority granted to the job-holder in order to achieve the expected results)

Duties:

1.
2.
3.
4.
5.
6.

(carried out by the job-holder and not delegated to a subordinate)

Contacts:

Internal (other than direct superior or subordinate)

External

Administration

In a way this can be considered as a neutral factor. Good administration will not necessarily result in strong motivation, but it will remove the obstacles to people doing their work effectively. Poor administration can, on the other hand, cause discontent and result in weak motivation. The aim of good administration in this context is to ensure that certain elements of a job are not allowed to give rise to frustration or discontent. These include:

Pay,
conditions of work,
procedure for introduction of the new employee to the firm,
clear understanding of what is expected of the individual,
freedom to get on with the job without irritating delays.

Pay calls for close attention from two points of view. First, the rate of pay for each job must be adequate, taking into account the demands of the job, pay for other jobs in the firm, and pay for like jobs in the district. A sense of grievance over pay can result in a poor effort from the individual. Secondly, wages and salaries must be paid promptly when due, and correctly. If any error is made in the amount paid it must be corrected as a first priority. Frequent mistakes in pay, and delays in rectifying them, can result in annoyance and suspicion in the friendliest of small companies.

Conditions of work should be as favourable as the circumstances of the firm can allow. The employees of the very small firm may very often accept conditions very much below the standard achieved by some large companies. They do so for a variety of reasons: perhaps they prefer the 'family' atmosphere; they might feel a loyalty to the boss; the freedom from strict rules and discipline might appeal to them; they might realise that the firm cannot yet afford to pay for better arrangements. But this does not mean that the owner of the business should ignore this aspect.

If possible, hours of work should be planned to suit the needs of people, as long as the needs of the business are met. Many firms of perhaps 5–20 employees have practised flexible working hours long before the idea was adopted in large firms and became fashionable.

The temperature and cleanliness of the work place and premises should be such that people find the place a congenial one to work in. Many small firms' standards in these respects are such that employees in larger firms would refuse to accept them. Sometimes they may hardly meet the statutory and local requirements.

Particular attention must be paid to the health and safety of employees at work. Apart from meeting current legal requirements, the owner should make frequent inspections to look for hazards that may cause accidents. Especially when machinery is being used, constant vigilance is needed to ensure that people are using equipment properly, that guards are always in place, that items of safety equipment such as eye protectors or safety footwear are always available and used when the job calls for them. Precautions against fire should be carefully designed: all employees should know what to do in case of fire. Apart from the human suffering involved, the firm's best interests cannot be served by injured or sick employees.

It is important when a new employee is recruited that he is told everything necessary about the firm to stimulate interest and to give the sense of security arising from knowledge of one's place in the unit. This will be easy when the first employee is taken on. In the day-to-day contacts between boss and employee it is likely that most relevant information about the company will pass in an informal way. But as the firm grows more procedures and systems will be developed, more employees will be taken on, and rules will be made governing the activities of people at work. Many firms have developed such rules and procedures, often in an *ad hoc* manner, even before the number of employees has reached double figures. At this stage the owner should prepare a check-list of what every employee ought to know. Then someone (it may be the owner or a trusted subordinate) should be given the responsibility of making sure the newcomer is fully conversant with the contents of the list.

We have already discussed the need for clear definitions of jobs. Failure to make sure the employee understands his role and duties can lead to misunderstanding, frustration and discontent. Allied to this is the frustration felt by the keen worker when work is held up because of some failure by the manager or other employees. This might be a lack of raw material or proper tools in the factory. It might be lack of a particular drawing because someone failed to make the necessary arrangements. It might arise from the failure of a person in providing the clerk with the information necessary to complete the pay roll. Proper organisation, planning and control of all the activities of the firm will help to reduce these sources of frustration. Lack of planning and control can result in chaos which removes the sense of purpose necessary for good morale.

Leadership

The person who has attended conscientiously to the administration of all matters concerning the people working in the concern will have made a good start to the task of getting people to work effectively. But it is unlikely that this alone is enough to get them to put in the full effort of which they are capable. In addition to having their affairs looked after competently, most people need to have a goal to aim for, or an example to follow. Good leadership provides this stimulus. Not only will the leader have a clear idea of his own aims for the small enterprise, but he will take steps to let the staff know what these aims are. He will make sure that every employee knows how he can help to achieve these aims. He will encourage each individual to take responsibility and take decisions within the limit of his job. At the same time he will encourage employees to offer ideas on how work should be carried out. He will listen and take action when the ideas are sound, and explain why action is not possible or advisable if that should be the case. Perhaps more important, the good leader will set the example he would like others to follow. The boss who is seen to be putting at least as much effort and time into the job as the employees are expected to put in is thereby setting a standard. If from the leader's actions it is clear the company comes first, with personal comfort and convenience a poor second, others will be encouraged to take a similar attitude. A word of warning is advisable however. Many owners of small firms cannot understand why their work-people sometimes regard as unimportant matters which they themselves see of major importance. It may be the job which used too much material, the quotation which was not posted in time to reach the potential customer, or the failure to send the purchase order out on time. It must be remembered that the personal objectives of the owner are different from theirs. The owner probably wants the business to succeed to meet personal ambitions and objectives. The employees, keen and conscientious as they may be, are more likely to look on their job as a satisfying way of earning enough money to do those things they want to do in their private lives.

It is part of any leader's job to encourage employees to prepare themselves for more responsible jobs. The prospect of advancement acts as a strong incentive to many people. This preparation may include formal training carried out internally in aspects of work at which the employee is not yet competent. It may include training within the firm such as the shopkeeper giving instruction to an assistant in the art of stock control, or the foreman in the factory providing the opportunity for the promising employee to acquire new skills. It may be allowing a person who appears to have the qualities required in a supervisor to take on some of the owner's work, with the support and guidance of the owner. Not only will this training increase the competence of employees and stimulate their interest, but the firm will be developing people for more senior positions as the firm grows.

When the firm has reached the stage when an employee has been promoted to a supervisory job it is important that he is allowed to get on with it. The owner will give this person every help and all the guidance needed. But having made the appointment the fact that this person is their new boss must be made clear to all members of the group over whom the new supervisor is to exercise authority. The owner must not give direct orders to the group other than through the supervisor except in matters of real urgency. Similarly, the members of the group will lose direct access to the owner for decisions on day-to-day operations. If this rule is not observed the morale of the supervisor will suffer and employees will have doubts as to who really is their boss. This does not mean that the owner and his employees no longer talk to each other. This is bound to happen in the normal course of the day's work, and the conscientious owner will in any event want to know what is going on, and how people feel about their work. One of the skills of management is to maintain this contact without interfering in the province of the supervisor.

To summarise, we may say that as soon as it is necessary to engage employees the owner must exercise the art of managing people by paying attention to the following aspects:

Legal requirements.
Selection.
Sound administration of all matters affecting employees.
Proper introduction of newcomers to the firm.
Leadership, including personal example.
Encouragement of initiative.
Development of people's abilities.

This may all appear to be common sense as indeed it is. Unhappily, it is in the small firm that, in the experience of the authors, the owner is often so busy that these aspects are often overlooked. But time must be found otherwise as the firm grows the enthusiasm of the employees will wane and grievances multiply. It may be too late to regain the initial good-will.

13 The Firm and the Law

All forms of business, sole traders, partnerships, limited companies, in retailing, services or manufacturing are constrained to some extent in their operations by national and local legislation. Although ignorance of the law is no defence, nevertheless the wise owner will not attempt to become an expert in legal matters, for two reasons. First, the time necessary to study the vast amount of legislation which exists could be better spent in making the firm profitable. Secondly, new laws are constantly being enacted, and existing ones amended or repealed so that no one, other than a specialist in legal matters, is able to keep up-to-date. It was for this reason we recommended earlier that before setting out in business a good commercial solicitor should be found to guide the firm in its efforts to keep within the law in its dealings with other people, companies or public bodies.

However, it is advisable for the owner of the small firm to know enough about the law to be able to recognise when legal advice or help is called for. The large company has its legal department, and its senior managers can leave legal matters to the experts; the managers of small firms have to fend for themselves.

The difficulty in writing on the subject in any great detail arises from the many, frequent changes in national and, to a lesser extent, local laws and regulations so that what is written is always in danger of rapidly becoming out-of-date. For this reason the most useful reference books on legal matters are issued in loose-leaf form and the publishers issue amendments at frequent intervals. What we shall attempt to do here is to give an outline of the more important aspects of the law, most of which are likely to remain either virtually unchanged, or with occasional amendments, for some time to come. It is impossible to cover all local regulations and bye-laws; the owner must consult the firm's solicitor, the local council officers or the local library for detailed local information.

It will probably help give a clearer view if we divide the legislation into four categories: (i) the firm and the customer; (ii) the firm and its employees; (iii) the firm and the state; and (iv) the firm and the community. At the end of this chapter a fuller list of current legislation is given as a guide to the owner who may want to pursue any particular aspect in more detail.

The Firm and the Customer

The basis of all business dealing is the contract. Whenever a person or firm agrees to supply goods or a service in exchange for some consideration (usually cash, but occasionally other goods or services) then in essence a legally enforceable contract exists. This assumes that both parties have the legal capacity to make the contract. An important point for the trader, especially the retailer, to bear in mind is that it is not possible to enforce a contract made with a person under the age of eighteen unless the goods are recognised in law as 'necessaries'. A contract need not be in writing; it can be spoken, or even implied. For example, the shopper who takes an article from the supermarket shelf and offers payment at the check-out makes a contract with the retailer when the offer of cash is accepted.

The main statute governing trade between the firm and the customer is the Sale of Goods Act 1979, which consolidates certain terms which are implied to be part of any contract. Some of the more important terms are outlined in the following paragraphs.

Any goods sold are deemed to be of merchantable quality unless any defects are drawn to the buyer's attention. However, if the buyer had examined the goods before the contract was made, and it is reasonable to assume that the defect would be discovered during the examination, the seller may thereby be relieved of this duty. If, in the absence of this disclosure or examination, any defect is subsequently found in the goods there is a breach of contract by the seller, and the buyer may take appropriate action to maintain his rights against the seller. If the goods are manufactured and sold through a wholesaler, retailer or other intermediary the buyer may also have rights against the manufacturer.

Goods must be fit for the purpose for which they are bought, provided that the buyer makes known the particular purpose. This does not apply however if the seller can prove that the buyer did not rely on the seller's skill, knowledge or judgment when the purchase was made.

It is possible to make a contract which expressly excludes some terms which would otherwise be implied by the Act. There are some terms however which may not be excluded and these are specified in the Unfair Contract Terms Act 1977. This is a complicated matter calling for the advice of a specialist.

A further limitation is placed on traders in the Fair Trading Act 1973. This Act restricts persons selling to the public from excluding their liability by exhibiting a sign which purports to exempt them from any responsibility for breach of contract. Such signs as 'No refunds', 'Goods not returnable', therefore, are unenforceable. Contracts between commercial firms, however, may contain exemption clauses to protect the seller, but when tested in the courts many such clauses have been declared to be invalid.

It is an offence for a trader to make any misleading or untrue statements when offering goods for sale, for example, by making false price comparisons. Some statements which are unlikely to mislead people may be overlooked, for example, 'We have the best bargains' or, 'only John Smith offers so much for so little'. The buyer who enters into a contract on the basis of a misrepresentation may legally repudiate the contract.

The Trades Description Act 1968 takes the matter further. Under this Act any trader who wilfully makes false or misleading statements about his product may, in addition to any civil action, have to face criminal charges. An everyday example of this is the retailer who displays goods at a certain price and then charges a higher price. In cases which are pursued in the courts compensation may be awarded to the buyer.

Another Act particularly relevant to the retailer is the Fair Trading Act 1973. Under this Act procedures are established whereby the Director-General of Fair Trading may investigate trading practices which may lead to customers being misled, or which misrepresent customers' rights (for example under guarantees) or lead them into transactions on inequitable terms or subject them to unfair pressure. The Director-General may require traders who he considers to be following such practices to give assurances for their future behaviour. In the absence of such assurance, or in the event of failure to honour the assurance, the Director-General may prosecute.

Anyone setting up a business in which arrangements will be made to arrange credit for consumers or to introduce consumers to sources of credit or cash (hire purchase houses are a good example of such sources) must first apply for a licence from the Office of the Director-General. This is laid down in the Consumer Credit Act 1974 which also defines the consumers' rights, the procedure by which the credit arrangements are made, and the methods which the supplier of credit may employ to exercise his rights or to enforce the provision made for security. If the firm intends to advertise the fact that credit arrangements are available it would be wise to consult the Consumer Credit (Advertisement) Regulation which sets standards which have to be met in such advertisements.

The Firm and its Employees

When a firm takes on its first employee (unless a close relative) it must notify the local office of the Department of Employment and thereby becomes subject to a range of legislation. When the number of employees increases to five the number of legal requirements also increases. Any firm having more than twenty employees is subject to the complete range of legislation dealing with employment of people. All these requirements are in addition to any other laws governing the relationships between individuals. The new employer should remember that when an offer of paid employment is made to a person, and that person accepts the offer, a contract exists whether or not the offer was made or accepted orally or in writing.

The legislation with which the employer will be most concerned covers three facets: (i) collective rights of employees; (ii) individual rights of employees; and (iii) health and safety.

The legislation covering the collective rights refers to the rights of employees to organise themselves in trade unions for the purpose of bargaining collectively with the employer. The new small firm is unlikely to find itself affected by this legislation. In most very small firms the relationship between the employees and the owner is such that the question of trade union organisation rarely arises. However, it is important to note that all employees have a right to join a recognised trade union and may not have this right excluded in any contract. Thus a contract which makes it a condition of employment that the employee does not join a union is invalid.

The small firm employer will be more concerned with the second and third categories. To deal with the second category – individual rights – first, the main Acts are the Employment Protection Act 1975, Equal Pay Act 1970, Sex Discrimination Act 1975, and Race Relations Act 1976. Some of the provisions of these Acts apply to the firm at the time that the first employee is engaged. For example, it is unlawful when selecting an employee to discriminate against any applicant on grounds of sex, race, or colour. This means that any advertisement placed in the press or elsewhere must not imply or state that only men or only women will be considered, or that members of certain races will be excluded.

When employees have been engaged women and men must be paid the same wages or salary for work of equal value, and must be given the same conditions of work, opportunities for training and opportunities for promotion. Similarly there must be no discrimination in these matters against people on grounds of race or colour.

A person who has worked for an employer for thirteen weeks must be given a written statement of the terms and conditions under which he is employed. This statement is sometimes wrongly described as a contract of employment. It may be drawn up and signed as a formal contract, but this is not necessary. The contract existed when the person was engaged. There are occasions when a formal contract is desirable to protect the employer; for example, if the firm is developing a new invention which the proprietor wishes to remain secret, the contract may contain clauses to protect the secrecy. But in general the normal statement meets the needs of both employee and employer.

The minimum information which is required in the statement, in addition to stating who the employer and employee are, comprises:

Date of starting as an employee
Rate of pay
Whether pay is daily, weekly, monthly, etc.
Conditions and hours of work
Holiday arrangements
Holiday pay
Pay during sickness or when recovering from injury
Details of pension schemes and whether contracted in, or contracted out of the State Pension Scheme
Notice to be given by the employee
Any rules regarding discipline in the firm
In the event of a grievance or complaint, the person to whom it must be made
Job title.

After an employee has worked with the firm for four weeks he is entitled to a week's notice of dismissal. After two years the period of notice extends to two weeks, and thereafter one week's extra notice is required for each year of service up to twelve years. So the maximum period of notice laid down in the Acts is twelve weeks.

Up to the end of the second year an employee in the very small firm may be dismissed for any reason. (There are certain exceptions – a person cannot be fairly dismissed at any time for trade union membership or activity, nor on grounds which contravene the laws against discrimination.) After that period he has a right not to be dismissed unfairly. If the firm has more than twenty employees this period is reduced to one year.

The main grounds on which an employee may be fairly dismissed after these periods are either lack of competence, inability for any other reason to perform the work, or the job itself becoming redundant. The latter term means that the work has been discontinued, or the volume of work has declined so that fewer people are required. Dismissal for any other reason might result in the employee claiming unfair dismissal at an Industrial Relations Tribunal, and reinstatement or compensation being awarded. It should be noted that if the employer's behaviour towards the employee is such that the latter feels compelled to leave, the employee may still claim that he has been unfairly dismissed. This is termed 'constructive dismissal'.

After an employee has worked for two years (this period is the same for all sizes of firm) and is then given notice to leave because the job has become redundant, the employer has to pay a lump sum as redundancy pay. The amount depends on the age and length of service of the employee; a percentage of this sum (currently 41 per cent) can then be reclaimed from a Redundancy Fund through the Department of Employment. A point to watch if the business is not starting from scratch, but has been bought as a going concern, is that any period the employees have served with the previous employer counts as service with the new employer. The new owner could therefore be inheriting a liability for several years' redundancy pay. This could be a serious matter if, after taking the business over, the new owner finds that fewer staff are needed, perhaps because of a change in the pattern of business or the introduction of more efficient working methods.

The other main feature of the Employment Protection Act of which the owner of the small firm should be aware is that concerning women who leave to have a baby. After two years' service, a woman has a right to a period of leave which can extend from twelve weeks before the expected date of the pregnancy to twenty-eight (or in special cases thirty-two weeks) after the birth of the child. After that period, providing that the woman has given proper notice as laid down in the Employment Protection Act, she is entitled to return to her old job or an equivalent one. The firm of less than five employees is freed from this commitment if it can be shown that it would be unreasonable to expect the firm to comply.

Health and Safety

There are three main Acts whose principal purpose is to ensure the health and safety of people at work. They are the Health and Safety at Work Act 1974, Factories Act 1961, and Offices, Shops and Railway Premises Act 1963. The Health and Safety at Work Act is a general Act which, in effect, says that every person in the firm has a legal responsibility for ensuring the health and safety of all people at work. Under this Act everyone – people who work in the workshop or clerks in the office, supervisors, managers and proprietors – may be prosecuted for committing any act or allowing an act to be committed which presents a threat to the health or safety of employees.

The owner of any firm having five or more employees must prepare and publish a statement of the firm's policy on matters of health and safety and ensure that all employees understand it. The matters which the statement must cover are detailed in the Act. When the firm reaches the stage where a trade union may be recognised the owner might find himself compelled to set up a safety committee, with special rights and powers as specified in the Act.

The Factories Act and the Offices, Shops and Railway Premises Act support the Health and Safety Act by spelling out in detail what firms must and must not do. There are some exceptions allowed for the self-employed or the firm where all employees are part-timers (working fewer than 21 manhours weekly). Most of the provisions however apply to all firms. Both Acts cover more or less the same ground including matters such as:

Lighting – this must be adequate to carry out work without strain.

Temperature – must be at least 16 °C after the first hour and a thermometer must be installed on every floor to check this. (A separate Order dealing with conservation of fuel lays down a maximum temperature of 19 °C.)

Overcrowding – each employee must have a working space at least 40 feet square and 400 cubic feet in volume.

Lavatory facilities – minimum scales are specified.

Drinking and washing water – rules for this depend on the type of work carried out.

Seating – if work can be done sitting down, employees must have seats provided, if not there must be enough seats available for them to sit down whenever the work does allow (e.g. in shops the scale is one for each three assistants).

First aid – minimum scales of equipment are specified depending on the number of employees.

Fencing of machines – all machinery must be suitably guarded.

Protective clothing and equipment – must be supplied when necessary and their use enforced.

Cleanliness – premises must be kept clean, and must be painted to specified standards at specified intervals.

Women and young persons – their hours of work are limited in number, and there are special rules about shift working and overtime. There is a legal minimum to the number of holidays to be given.

Fire – premises where more than twenty people are employed (or more than ten on any upper floor) must have a Fire Certificate.

In addition to these general requirements there are other Acts or Regulations relating to individual industries, especially those concerned with dangerous chemicals, explosives, mining and other dangerous activities or substances.

The Acts are enforced by the Health and Safety Inspectorate through a network of regional offices carrying a staff of inspectors. These inspectors may demand entry to any premises at any reasonable time without warning, and are empowered to carry out any inspection they think fit. They may give advice, insist on improvements, order processes to be stopped, and even prosecute the owner and any of the employees for failing in their duty of preserving health and ensuring safety.

One aspect of these Acts will affect the owners of most manufacturing firms even before any work is started. That is the requirement that any person intending to operate a power-driven machine must notify the local inspector before it may be used. It is a criminal offence not to do so.

Little has been said about rates of pay, hours of work and holidays. This is because there is no general legislation on the subject. The government has always preferred to leave these matters to be negotiated between employers and employees. There are, however, two important exceptions to this general rule. One has already been mentioned – the hours of work and holidays of women and young persons. The other exception is that some trades and industries have their wages and conditions decreed by Wages Councils. These are bodies set up by the government when it has appeared necessary to protect employees who are not able to organise themselves to bargain collectively with employers. There are inspectors whose duty it is to visit establishments operating in these industries to ensure that the minimum wages and conditions are being observed.

The Firm and the State

Some of the requirements concerning the relationship between firm and state have already been dealt with. The Companies Act, Partnership Acts and the Industrial and Friendly Societies Acts lay down the legal framework within which the firm may work. The sole trader should note that while there is no specific Act to cover this form of business there is at least one relevant reference in the Companies Act. This is the requirement already mentioned that all businesses, whether incorporated or not, must display the names of the owner(s) on stationery and in the business premises.

The other important aspect is that of taxation. All profits are subject to tax, and one of the aims of any commercial venture is to avoid paying more tax than is required by law. Many owners become so engrossed with the question of tax that they devote an excessive amount of time to it – time which should be spent in activities aimed at increasing profit. This is something which is best left to the expert, the accountant or solicitor. Other taxes on which the owner may wish to seek advice are capital gains tax and capital transfer tax both of which could be very important to the small family business. The subject is complicated and warrants an expert's attention.

Because corporation tax is levied at a different rate from personal tax it sometimes happens that there is a tax saving in moving from sole trader or partnership to limited company status. This again is a matter on which expert advice is needed.

Finally, all employers must pay National Insurance contributions and also take out Employers' Liability Insurance. (These are dealt with in chapter 14.)

The Firm and the Community

Many of the Acts already discussed also affect the relationship of the firm to other people and organisations. The Health and Safety at Work Act states that firms must not undertake any activity which would endanger the health or safety of *any* person whether inside or outside the premises. Further, when people other than employees are on the firm's premises or work site the firm must take positive action to ensure their health and safety. This might include supplying protective clothing and equipment such as goggles and helmets.

The Act also stipulates that designers, manufacturers, importers and others involved in putting a product on the market are responsible for the safety of the equipment which they supply, when it is used properly. This could have important implications, for example, for the inventor of a new piece of industrial or domestic equipment. To avoid infringing the law it is advisable to make sure that not only are the goods safe but that adequate instructions are issued for their proper use. A similar comment applies to the importer – many operating instructions which accompany imported goods are unclear and inadequate.

Other Acts restrict the liberty of the firm to pollute the atmosphere, create unnecessary noise, or allow noxious materials to be discharged to the danger or inconvenience of the public. Any owner who feels that the firm's activities might have effects of this nature should seek expert advice. Penalties can be quite severe and the firm could be compelled to cease operations.

The Shop Acts, 1950–65 impose restrictions on the hours during which shops may open. As a general rule they may open for six days a week and close all day on Sunday and on one other afternoon from 1.00 pm. Shops may not be open after 8.00 pm (or 9.00 pm on Saturdays). There are many exceptions to these rules. Late opening is permitted for example to restaurants and cafés, or shops selling nearly-cooked foods or medicines. Garages selling petrol or motor accessories are also exempt. Sunday opening is permitted if the proprietor, because of his religious faith, observes Saturday as the holiday and closes the shop on that day.

The Offices, Shops and Railway Premises Act dictates certain standards of cleanliness which have to be observed on premises where food is handled. The premises must be clean and free from damp, temperatures must be controlled to an appropriate level, and the shop assistants must be clean and must not smoke near food.

One special relationship to consider is that between landlord and tenant. The firm might be leasing its property, or it might be letting some unwanted part of its own premises to a tenant. In either event the tenancy will be subject to the landlord and Tenant Act 1954. By virtue of this Act, when a business lease expires the tenant has a right to a new lease at the expiry of the current one. However, there are circumstances in which the landlord may successfully oppose the application for renewal. One such valid reason is that the landlord needs the premises for his own business. When the lease is not renewed the tenant is usually entitled to compensation based on the rateable value of the premises.

In addition to this national legislation there are, of course, local regulations to be complied with. Important aspects which may come into this category are: Planning permission – new premises or changes of use; Fire regulations – there may be local regulations in addition to national laws; and Inspection of food shops.

Sources of Information

Fortunately, there are sources of information on several aspects of the law which are available to the layman, in addition to the Acts themselves (published by HMSO) and, of course, the firm's solicitor. Employment legislation is particularly well covered. There are publications written in non-legal language and issued in loose-leaf form which cover the subject thoroughly. They are amended regularly to keep up-to-date with latest legislation and amendments. The best known is probably *Croner's Guide to Employers* published by Croner Publications.

There is also an excellent series of leaflets available free from any Job Centre under the title *Employment Protection*. (In most recent leaflets the title has changed to *Employment Legislation*.)

The Department of Employment issue a publication monthly entitled *Employment Gazette* (this is not free). There are also many other pamphlets and leaflets issued by the Department of Employment. The list is too long to include here, but the local offices of the Department should be able to provide details of all that are available.

Many people are unaware of the free services offered by the Advisory, Conciliation and Arbitration Service (ACAS). In addition to its more widely publicised role as a conciliator, ACAS has staff available to give sound advice on most matters concerning management of employees. There is an ACAS office in many cities and towns.

The Health and Safety Executive issue a series of free booklets dealing with the Health and Safety at Work Act. They are available at local offices of the Executive. In addition, individual inspectors are usually prepared to give advice on any problems.

On legal matters in general, advice is always available to firms which have joined an appropriate organisation. Examples of these bodies are: Chambers of Commerce, Employers' Federations, and Trade Associations, and there is always the local library available with its store of information. A useful loose-leaf publication which helps business people to keep up-to-date is the *Company Secretary's Review* published by Tolley Publishers. Advice on local rules and regulations and on measures to comply with them may be obtained from: town halls, council offices, fire authorities, local health authorities and council members.

The prospective owner of a business will have gathered from this brief account that the amount of legislation affecting the average firm is very large. Nevertheless, firms do manage to cope and survive by taking proper advice at the right time and making use of all the information, free and otherwise, which is available.

Legislation of Interest to the Smaller Business

You and your customers

Consumer Credit Act 1974
Consumer Protection Acts 1961, 1971
Consumer Safety Act 1978
Fair Trading Act 1973
Food and Drugs Act 1955
Sales of Goods Act 1979
Supply of Goods (Implied Terms) Act 1973
Trade Descriptions Acts 1968, 1972
Unfair Contract Terms Act 1977
Weights and Measures Acts 1963, 1979

Your and your employees

Employers Liability (Compulsory Insurance) Act 1969
Employment Act 1980
Employment and Training Act 1973
Employment Protection Act 1975
Employment Protection (Consolidation) Act 1978
Equal Pay Act 1970

Factories Act 1961
Health and Safety at Work Act 1974
Industrial Training Act 1964
Offices, Shops and Railway Premises Act 1963
Race Relations Act 1976
Redundancy Payments Act 1965
Sex discrimination Act 1975
Trade Union and Labour Relations Act 1974
Wages Councils Act 1979

You and the state / local government
Companies Acts 1948–1981
Control of Pollution Act 1974
European Communities Act 1972
Income and Corporation Taxes Act 1970
Partnership Act 1890
Redundancy Payments Act 1977
Shops Acts 1950–1965
Social Security Act 1975, 1979
Social Security Pensions Act 1975
Finance Acts (annual)
Local fire and other regulations

You and your landlord/tenant
Landlord and Tenant Act 1954
Rent Act 1977

There may also be local or national restrictions on particular types of activity, for which you must seek a licence and/or planning permission. Note also the possible effects of the provisions of the Treaty of Rome on UK legislation.

14 Insurance

Before starting to trade the prudent owner will take out insurances against the different misfortunes which the business may meet in the course of trading, and which could result in serious harm to the business. The importance of ensuring that the insurance cover is adequate cannot be over-emphasised; many firms which have underinsured are now out of business.

The subject may be considered under two headings: voluntary insurance and insurance to meet statutory requirements. Among the insurance policies which should be taken voluntarily are the following.

Fire – this is probably one of the major causes of heavy loss in many businesses. The retailer could lose his premises and stock; the manufacturer may lose buildings, plant and equipment, fixtures and fittings and stocks of both raw materials, work in progress and finished goods. The important point to bear in mind is that the insurance should cover the cost of reinstating or replacing these assets at current costs not at historical cost.

Flood and other natural hazards – the losses due to these causes may perhaps not be on the same scale as those caused by a serious fire, but the same principles apply; insure for reinstatement value.

Consequential loss – even when the cover for replacement of fixed assets may be adequate, the other consequences of the fire, flood, etc. must not be overlooked. Additional expenses may be incurred for such items as site clearance, professional fees, wages and salaries of employees whom the employer wishes to retain to be available when business resumes.

Loss of profit – in the event of any major hold-up of business for any length of time, due to fire, flood, etc., there will probably be a serious loss of profit. Insurance can be taken out to compensate for such losses.

Burglary – losses due to burglary can cause more loss than the value of goods stolen. Damage could be caused to locks, doors, windows, filing cabinets, fixtures and fittings, office and workshop machinery. It will therefore be prudent to cover for these other possibilities fully.

Cash in transit – if it will be the practice to carry or allow employees to carry cash from the premises to the bank (for example, the retailer's takings) or to carry cash from the bank to the premises (for example, wages) a policy should be taken out to cover any losses incurred during the journey. The need for this cover may be reduced by agreeing with employees to pay their wages by cheque or direct transfer.

Bad debts – if the business is one which will be giving credit in the course of trade it is possible to insure against bad debts. Such insurance must be part of a well-thought out policy for credit control covering all the facets mentioned in the section on that subject.

Plate glass – the retailer or any other business having a show window will need cover for breakage of plate glass, replacement of which can be very costly.

Personal accident – it is well worth taking out insurance for any injuries which key personnel may sustain and which may prevent them from attending to the affairs of the business.

Other personal insurance – it is also advisable, especially in the partnership where all members are active and essential participants in the day-to-day running of the firm, to insure the firm against the loss of the services of any of these people arising from long illness or, even more importantly, death, because the death of a partner automatically leads to dissolution of the partnership. This in turn will mean that the capital and current account of the deceased partner will have to be repaid to his estate.

Vehicle insurance – this item comes into both categories, voluntary and obligatory. It is of course compulsory to insure against third party claims. It is prudent in addition to consider a comprehensive policy to cover damage to or loss of the vehicle. If a considerable amount of the business requires the carrying of goods, insurance should be taken out to compensate for loss of goods in transit. One point sometimes overlooked is that if a privately registered vehicle is to be used for carrying goods the policy must also cover this use, so it should be adjusted accordingly.

Professional negligence – the business might be one in which professional advice is given to customers. If so, it is possible and often desirable to take out insurance against any claim for losses or damage which are alleged to have been suffered as a result of the advice being acted upon.

Insurance Required by Law

There are three main forms of compulsory insurance: public liability insurance, employers liability insurance, and national insurance.

Public liability – a policy must be taken out against injury to people other than employees. Injuries might be caused on the premises – an example is a blow from a falling load. But they could also be sustained near to the premises, perhaps a loose load falling and striking a passer-by.

Employers' liability – all employers must cover against liability for personal injury and disease sustained by their employees, arising out of their employment. Although the Social Security Act 1975 requires the employer to pay national insurance (see next paragraph) this does not remove the legal duty to effect employers' liability insurance as well. Most policies issued give unlimited cover but otherwise the insurance taken out should be at least £2 million.

National insurance – there are different requirements for the self-employed person and for the business having employees. Self-employed persons are required to pay contributions, details of which may be obtained from the local office of the Department of Health and Social Security. The subject is rather complex as the amount and method of payment depends on the level of earnings of the self-employed persons, or on the profit or gains (chargeable to income tax) arising from the trade, profession or vocation.

Employers are required to pay a national insurance contribution for each employee. (This is in addition to the employee's contribution which the employer is compelled to deduct from wages and salaries, and pay to the Inland Revenue with the PAYE deductions.) The amount to be deducted is a fixed percentage of gross earnings if the employer has not contracted out of the state scheme. Employers who have contracted out pay a different percentage. This employer's contribution helps to fund the social security system, and includes a contribution to the maternity pay fund and the redundancy fund.

If any employer has any doubt at all about the payments to be made under this legislation it is important to get sound advice either from professional advisers or the government department concerned. Unlike voluntary insurance, failure to pay the correct compulsory insurance could lead to prosecution.

15 A Management Audit

During the early days of a new business the owner and his staff will almost certainly be preoccupied with day-to-day matters, developing systems and methods of working, meeting customers' needs, and dealing with unexpected difficulties. The result is that the manager has no time to stop and think. However, if the business is to prosper it is important that at some stage someone should step back and look at what has been achieved, how current performance compares with the targets set, and what action should be taken in the future to meet the objectives of the business.

If the advice in early chapters has been taken there will have been a regular series of reports on the financial results achieved, and these will have shown whether results are better than planned, worse than planned, or exactly on target. If better, the progressive entrepreneur will wish to identify the reason so that future action may exploit any opportunities revealed. If worse than planned, the reasons, when identified, should lead to remedial action. If the target has been met it is still desirable to ask what improvements can be made.

In order to identify possible sources of improvement many managers have found it useful to make time available at regular intervals to carry out, in a systematic way, a thorough survey of all aspects of their businesses. This survey enables an objective assessment to be made of the effectiveness of the operations, and points to the need for action in the future. In the same way that the accountant audits the financial practices these managers are in effect auditing the management practices and procedures of their businesses.

A useful aid to this management audit is a check-list covering all the important factors which affect the running of the business. In the following pages a suggested lay-out for a check-list is illustrated, but each business will have different needs and each person will draw up a list appropriate to the needs of the particular business.

	Review period			
	End of first	Then every		
	6 months	3 months	6 months	12 months
Personal				
Objectives	*			*
Involvement	*			*
Delegation	*			*
Control procedures				
Financial				
– profit	*		*	
– cash	*		*	
– debtors	*	*		
– creditors	*	*		
Production				
– customer service	*		*	
– use of plant	*		*	
– use of people	*		*	
– use of materials	*		*	
Stock				
– levels	*			*
– availability	*	*		
Marketing				
– size of market	*			*
– share of market	*			*
– selling methods	*			*
– promotion practices	*			*
– distribution	*			*
Production and Technical				
– type of equipment	*			*
– lay-out of plant	*			*
– methods of working	*			*
– maintenance of plant	*			*
– design of product	*			*
Materials and finished goods				
– buying	*		*	
– receipt	*		*	
– inspection	*		*	
– storage	*			*
– issue	*		*	

	Review period			
	End of first 6 months	Then every 3 months	6 months	12 months
Employees				
– job descriptions	*		*	
– delegation	*		*	
– pay policy	*		*	
– conditions of working	*		*	
– training	*		*	
The office				
– equipment	*			*
– aids	*			*
– procedures	*		*	
Premises				
– adequacy	*			*
– size	*			*
– lay-out	*			*
– access	*			*
– maintenance	*		*	
– services	*		*	
Legal matters				
– health and safety	*			*
– employment, tax, national insurance	*			*
– others	*			*
Advisers				
– accountant	*			*
– solicitor	*			*
Insurance	*			*

In the check-list illustrated, provision is made for a review at the end of the first six months and subsequently every three months. However, it will be noted that it is not proposed that everything should be reviewed every three months. Some items may not need reviewing more frequently than every six months or every twelve months; in the list this is indicated by an asterisk (*) in the appropriate column.

Using the Check-list

Most of the questions which the owner or manager should ask under the various headings will probably have become obvious during the preparation of the check-list, and other questions will be prompted when reading the relevant sections of this book. The following paragraphs indicate the kind of thinking which is desirable when carrying out such a review.

Personal

Under this heading the owner would review his own contribution to the business, and whether or not personal objectives were being met through the business. He might ask whether he is devoting enough of his own energies and time to the business, or, on the other hand, whether he is carrying out tasks which ought to be delegated to others.

Control procedures

There are certain questions which need to be asked about all control procedures:

Are they based on clear targets and plans?
Is the necessary information being provided?
Does this information lead to effective action, either to seize opportunities or to correct deficiencies?

Marketing

All the questions raised in the chapter on marketing need to be asked at frequent intervals, especially those concerning customers, selling methods and promotional activities.

Production

As the business grows (and this applies particularly to the manufacturing business) there may be a need for better equipment or machines accompanied by a review of the way the plant is laid out. it is almost certain that later *ad hoc* additions of plant and machines will have resulted in a less than ideal arrangement, no matter how well the workshop was laid out in the first place. Methods of working and methods of maintenance of plant and buildings would also come under scrutiny.

Materials and finished goods
The review would cover the adequacy of procedures, and particularly of the discipline exercised, at all stages from ordering raw materials to the final despatch of finished goods to the customer.

Employees
At some stage in the growth of the business it will be instructive to draw a simple diagram of the organisation to show how the various jobs relate to each other. This should lead to questions concerning the effectiveness of the way that responsibilities and authority have been delegated. It is equally important to keep in mind the need to maintain a high morale and to check that such matters as pay policy, working conditions and training policy are not having an adverse effect.

The office
Although the office is likely to be small and simple, it can play a vital part in the effective operation of the business. Some important questions are:

How well does the office provide the service which the rest of the business needs?
Is the manager satisfied that the office portrays a professional and business like image?
Is it difficult to find important papers?
Do things get lost?

The answers to these questions might well lead to changes in methods of working and perhaps to the adoption of improved equipment and aids.

Premises
While it is unlikely that the business will be making frequent changes of premises it is well to keep under review the factors suggested in the check-list. Are the premises adequate to the purposes of the

business? Are they too large or too small? Are there good means of access and exit for goods coming in and going out? Are maintenance costs unreasonably high? Are the services (electricity, gas etc.) adequate?

Legal matters

Has the business met all its legal obligations? In particular have the requirements of the Health and Safety at Work Act been met not only in regard to employees and other persons, but also to products which the firm has supplied to customers? In addition to these questions it is important to remember the legal requirements affecting pay and deductions from pay.

Advisers

The owner will need to check that the accountant is providing all the information essential to the proper management of the business as well as complying with statutory requirements. The value of the service provided by the solicitor in dealing with commercial, personnel and other related matters must be assessed. It is also worth asking whether enough use has been made of free advice, including such bodies as the Small Firms Centres, the Advisory Conciliation and Arbitration Service and the Health and Safety Executive.

Insurance

The questions here relate to adequacy of cover in the event of some untoward happening which may harm the business such as fire, floods, loss of valuable employee or partner, and the many other hazards which the business may have to face. It is important to check that the company is covered adequately for loss of profit as well as for the more obvious losses incurred.

Taking Action

It may not be practicable to make all the improvements suggested by the audit immediately. Where it is proposed to take action it is useful to impose a further measure of self-discipline by setting a target date for completion and to make a simple plan to meet that date. Where it is decided to postpone action the audit will have served to point out possible areas for improvement later on and this will be of value in any longer-term planning which the owner wishes to undertake.

Appendix 1
Useful Addresses

The Institute of Cost & Management Accountants
63 Portland Place
London W1N 4DB

The Association of Certified Accountants
29 Lincoln's Inn Fields
London WC2A 3EE

The Institute of Chartered Accountants in England and Wales
Chartered Accountants' Hall
Moorgate Place
London EC2P 2BJ

The Institute of Chartered Accountants of Scotland
27 Queens Street
Edinburgh
Scotland EH2 1LA

The Cooperative Development Agency
20 Albert Embankment
London SE1 7TJ

Department of Industry
Small Firms Division
219 Ashdown House
123 Victoria Street
London SW1E 6RB

Department of Industry
Small Firms Centre
53 Stephenson Street
Birmingham 2

Small Firms Service
Department of Industry
57 Bothwell Street
Glasgow G2 6TU

Small Firms Service
Department of Industry
16 St. David's House
Wood Street
Cardiff CF1 1ER

The Department of the Environment
2 Marsham Street
London SW1P 3EB

The Development Commission
11 Cowley Street
London SW1P 3NA

Council for Small Industries in Rural Areas
141 Castle Street
Salisbury
Wiltshire SP1 1EX

The National Enterprise Board
12–18 Grosvenor Gardens
London SW1W ODW

Welsh Office Industry Department
Gwydyr House,
Whitehall
London SW1

Development Corporation of Wales
Cwmbran Development Corporation
Gwent House, Town Centre
Cwmbran, Gwent

Development Board for Rural Wales
Ladywell House
Newtown
Powys SY16 1JB

Scottish Economic Planning Department
(Industrial Division)
New St. Andrews House
St. James's Centre
Edinburgh

Highlands & Islands Development Board
Bridge House
Bank Street
Inverness IV1 1QR

Scottish Development Agency
New St. Andrews House
St. James's Centre
Edinburgh

Northern Ireland Development Agency
Maryfield
100 Belfast Road
Holywood
C. Down BT18 9QX
Northern Ireland

Local Enterprise Development Unit
Lamont House
Purdy's Lane
Newtownbreda
Belfast BT8 4TD

Department of Commerce
Chichester House
64 Chichester Street
Belfast BT1 4JX

Patent Office and Industrial Property and Copyright Department
25 Southampton Buildings
Chancery Lane
London WC2A 1AY

Advisory Conciliation and Arbitration Service
Cleland House
Page Street
London SW1P 4ND

Health & Safety Executive
Caxton House
Tothill Street
London SW1H 9NA

Department of Employment
Caxton House
Tothill Street
London SW1H 9NA

British Overseas Trade Board
1 Victoria Street
London SW1H OET

British Standards Institution
British Standards House
2 Park Street
London W1A 2BS

The Law Society
113 Chancery Lane
London WC2

Croner's Publications Ltd
Croner House
173 Kingston Road
New Malden
Surrey

Tolley Publishing Company Ltd
209 High Street
Croydon CRO 1QR

Acknowledgements

The authors gratefully acknowledge the assistance so willingly given by David Boden, MSc and Dennis Redden, FCMA, FCCA, MIMC, whose comments and suggestions during the writing of the books were very valuable.

Index